PRAISE FOR RON GEREVAS AND *CHANGE AGENT*

For nearly twenty years, I've had the privilege of working with Ron Gerevas in the CSUSM College of Business Administration. He recognized that career and professional development was the most critical and missing piece of the college's curriculum. Drawing upon his own impressive career, he succeeded in transforming an optional career class into the mandatory Business Professional Development career course of the Business School. In addition to teaching and coaching, Ron chaired the college's Board of Directors, which helped chart the course for the college as well as served on the university's Foundation Board, which helped guide, advise, and support the entire university for nine years.

Our students are incredibly fortunate to have Ron's impact on their lives and careers, as am I.

—JIM HAMERLY
Former dean, College of Business Administration at California State University San Marcos

Ron believes deeply in helping our veterans transition into meaningful career jobs after their service to our country. I've witnessed his leadership skills and dedication to accomplishing his mission. He has been a great mentor to veterans and advisor to the leadership of the university on their military affiliates. *Change Agent* is a must-read for veterans.

—TONY JACKSON
MajGen, USMC (Ret); past director and chairman, CSUSM Foundation Board

Ron's "Ten Career Commandments" work wonders, regardless of where you are in your career. I should know. I recently published my own book in which I publicly stated he is the only boss I've ever had whom I learned from and respected. He personally helped me start my own successful executive search firm, and later I continued to rely on his commandments as my foundation during a complete rebrand. His book will inspire you to achieve more than you ever thought possible.

—KEN SCHMITT

CEO and founder, TurningPoint Executive Search;
author, The Practical Optimist

Ron is a visionary leader who transformed the executive search industry. Seeing the need for greater specialization, he pioneered new business models that reshaped global firms like Heidrick & Struggles and Spencer Stuart. Ron had the courage to challenge the status quo and implement innovative practices to better serve clients. His passion for raising industry standards lifted all boats. I know; I was one who benefited from his industry leadership and change. I built my own successful executive search firm in line with his innovations, which he later acquired as CEO of Heidrick & Struggles. I know him and his work well.

You, too, will benefit from his sage advice and formula for success. *Change Agent* is a must-read.

—TOM MITCHELL

Founder and CEO, TMLZ Executive Search; former Senior partner,
Heidrick & Struggles

I have been blessed to know Ron Gerevas throughout my career as a friend and as a guide to understanding the complexity of human relations in the workplace. I am thrilled that Ron is bringing forward to a global audience the deep insights that have made him one of the world's most respected executive recruiters and a business and life coach to countless leaders of industry.

—SANDY CLIMAN

Founder and CEO, Entertainment Media Ventures, Inc.; former executive vice president and president, Worldwide Business Development, Universal Studios; former talent agent and senior executive, Creative Artists Agency

I've known Ron for over twenty years and observed his relentless quest for excellence and his vision for strategic change. Having practiced corporate leadership and taught college career courses, like Ron, I can tell you that *Change Agent* is an innovative blueprint for anyone who is ready and willing to reach their potential at work and in life. Coupled with his wisdom of finding purpose and successfully directing change that impacted three different industries, this book is an important read.

—DAVID BENNETT

(Ret) Senior executive, Pepsico/Taco Bell; Marriott/Host International; Mail Boxes, Etc.; Worldwide; and college professor

I've known Ron since he achieved enough on our college campus to earn him Outstanding Graduate. Then I had a front row seat, watching him display the same leadership skills in our first job after graduate school at J. Walter Thompson Advertising in New York City. Within a year, he received two promotions and was congratulated on achieving the fastest top management track ever at the biggest ad agency in the world. From there his career only got better.

Change Agent reveals Ron's incredible journey of success and how you can exceed your career expectations through authenticity, innovation, and compassion. His lifetime devotion to changing things for the better included personally encouraging me to start my own advertising agency using a specialization model. My daughter now runs our successful family ad agency.

—WAYNE NELSON

Founder and CEO, Nelson & Gilmore Advertising; former J. Walter Thompson executive

CHANGE AGENT

RON GEREVAS

CHANGE AGENT

THE ART AND ADVENTURE OF RELENTLESS CAREER INNOVATION

Advantage | Books

Published by Advantage Books, Charleston, South Carolina.
An imprint of Advantage Media.

ADVANTAGE is a registered trademark, and the Advantage colophon is a trademark of Advantage Media Group, Inc.

Printed in the United States of America.

10 9 8 7 6 5 4 3 2 1

ISBN: 978-1-64225-899-8 (Hardcover)
ISBN: 978-1-64225-898-1 (eBook)

Library of Congress Control Number: 2023923223

Cover design by Matthew Morse.
Layout design by Megan Elger.

This publication is designed to provide accurate and authoritative information in regard to the subject matter covered. It is sold with the understanding that the publisher is not engaged in rendering legal, accounting, or other professional services. If legal advice or other expert assistance is required, the services of a competent professional person should be sought.

Advantage Books is an imprint of Advantage Media Group. Advantage Media helps busy entrepreneurs, CEOs, and leaders write and publish a book to grow their business and become the authority in their field. Advantage authors comprise an exclusive community of industry professionals, idea-makers, and thought leaders. For more information go to **advantagemedia.com**.

My grandfather, PaPa Joe, was my compass for life. He taught me the importance of changing things for the better and why my life would be better for doing it.

CONTENTS

ACKNOWLEDGMENTS

Thanks to my mother for her love, for pushing me to make the most out of my life, and for instilling in me a competitive spirit to be a winner: to never give up, and never stop trying.

Thanks to Dean Stanley Benz for my career wake-up call and advice. Thanks to Jack Holland for introducing me to advertising and for recommending J. Walter Thompson as a target company to join after graduate school. Thanks to Bill Boggie for being my closest friend and roommate throughout most of college and sharing so many wonderful memories.

My transition into New York and JWT went well thanks to my dear friend Mike Hooper. Steve Smith and Phil Mygatt, who are no longer with us, were responsible for my rapid growth and leadership development at JWT. They were the first to recognize my future as a change agent.

I want to thank Mike Balzano for first teaching me how to get things done in Washington, DC and for elevating me into positions that allowed me to make major improvements in the Peace Corps and our country's domestic volunteer programs. I'll always be grateful to President Gerald Ford for allowing me to serve as one of his appointees.

There are four colleagues I especially want to thank for making my twenty-five years at Heidrick & Struggles so enjoyable and successful. Rick Nelson and Conrad Prusak were instrumental in helping me create the new business model and strategic plan that turned around the firm. Tom Mitchell and I grew up together in search. I will never be able to thank him enough for being my close friend and colleague. Thirty years of thanks to my executive assistant, Elaine Koutris, who was the only person who was with me throughout all of H&S and SS. Thanks, E.

I'd like to thank Tom Neff and Dayton Ogden for allowing me to help them at Spencer Stuart. It wasn't easy to hire the former CEO of your major competitor in executive search, but they did.

I want to thank David Bennett for bringing me to the College of Business Administration (CoBA) at CSUSM and for making it possible for me to teach. I want to thank Dean Jim Hamerly for his leadership and support in allowing me to elevate my career class into the crown jewel mandatory class of the Business School. Their mentoring and support meant a great deal to me.

I want to thank two of my closest friends, Pepper de Callier and Bill Hixson, who left this earth too early and whom I miss terribly. Each made me a better person, and I would like to think I did the same for them. If they were here today, we would surely be changing something.

Thanks to my friend and former colleague, Ken Schmitt, for encouraging me to write a book, and to Ezra Byer for helping me write it. Ezra was an absolute joy to learn from and work with.

And last but certainly not least is my family. I want to thank my children for making me a proud dad. I will always love them unconditionally. I can't even begin to thank the love of my life, Rosalie, for the past fifty-seven years. I can honestly say that this book would only be a short essay without her.

FOREWORD

Options and change are good. Embrace them.
—RON GEREVAS

At a very young age, Ron Gerevas had a mantra and a vision of what he wanted to achieve in his lifetime. His self-awareness and self-taught approach for each stage of life and opportunity propelled him forward. At his core was a mindset of service and a legacy of leaving everything he touched better than he found it.

He came from very humble beginnings, and his career journey is nothing short of spectacular, from being the first in his family to receive a college degree, to a successful advertising career on Madison Avenue, to being a presidential appointee for the Ford administration, and finally to an industry-leading career in executive search. Now, in his later years, his focus is on teaching and mentoring, helping both students embarking on their career journey and veterans transitioning from military to civilian life.

Throughout his career, he approached his personal life with a similar degree of dedication and focus, enjoying a marriage of nearly sixty years, raising two children, and participating in multiple marathons and triathlons around the world—even in his eighties. He also managed to become an award-winning winemaker along the way.

You might be reading this book because you have worked with Ron. Perhaps you have been his student or mentee. Or you know someone who knows him and has benefited from their connection or being a part of one of the organizations he's impacted.

I know him because he is my father, and while he has been a role model for so many, he and my mom have been a north star for my brother and me. His relentless work ethic, unquestioned integrity, unwavering focus on family, and approach to health, balance, and wellness have been key tenets for our lives.

With the core belief that options are good, and that understanding yourself and your strengths are key, Ron has helped shepherd colleagues, leaders, and organizations to be open to and embrace the change that was needed to save their market position and propel their organization forward.

I am a communications leader, currently at Qualcomm in San Diego, who prides herself on impacting the executive experience as much as the employee experience. I can attribute my confidence in managing teams and working with executives in part to the way I was raised. With business discussions around the dinner table and helping my parents host their annual holiday parties at our house for the Heidrick & Struggles Los Angeles office, I absolutely loved being part of the conversation and included in building connections at a young age.

I've known all along how fortunate I've been to have the best career coach and dad on the planet, through all stages of my life, cheering me on from the sidelines. I've learned how to have a big picture, strategic approach; how to embrace change and new opportunities; and the importance of cultivating relationships. But in my opinion, the most important lesson has been the perspective of being accountable and leaving everything you touch better than when you started.

I know you will enjoy learning about my dad's amazing journey and think, *Wow, what a man and what a wonderful life*. He has written an interesting and important book, sharing helpful tools and an empowering perspective. You may find an entirely new approach to life or, at the very least, glean some nuggets from his innovative career changes, no matter what stage of life you are in.

Happy reading.
MICHELLE A. GEREVAS

INTRODUCTION

hange whatever you touch. This is a principle that has marked my life for over half a century, and it's a model I've practiced throughout my career and in my personal life.

I've been a top leader in five different global organizations, which were all pillars in their industries. In four, I helped create and implement new business models that changed the historical direction and, in some cases, the entire industry for the better. I've been responsible for projects and staff reporting to me in over one hundred countries, six different continents, and all fifty US states. I've made speeches and presentations in the White House, in the US Senate, and around the globe.

I've walked away from positions others would consider the opportunity of a lifetime. These roles include the chief of staff to the vice president of the United States, the director of the creative department of one of the most respected advertising agencies in the world, the CEO/president of the National Restaurant Association in Washington, DC, and president of the most prestigious art design school in the world.

For the past fifteen years, I have coached and taught over a thousand university business school students at California State University San Marcos (CSUSM) on how to build a successful career in today's corporate world. In the process, I turned my elective college course into the crown jewel of the business school.

Of all my personal accomplishments, the ones that might mean the most to you, the reader, are my thirty-plus years in the executive search industry. During this extended period, I served as president and CEO of Heidrick & Struggles and vice chairman of Spencer Stuart. If you're an aspiring leader, no doubt these two names are on your radar screen. After all, they have been listed within the top five global executive search firms in the world since the industry was founded. This $30 billion industry is the gateway to filling most of the senior executive roles in all major companies that are not promoted from within. Both of these firms evaluate, recruit, process, and place executives all over the world.

In each company, I led the creation and implementation of revolutionary new business models. At Heidrick & Struggles, I was elected CEO and president by the partnership to create a three-year strategic plan and new business model. After dropping from first to fifth in world rankings and facing further decline, they needed someone to make significant improvements. I had been a partner in the firm for years and was very familiar with the ins and outs of how they operated. As Los Angeles office manager, I had already experimented with a very successful new model. And a few years later, Spencer Stuart brought me on board as vice chairman to incorporate much of what I had implemented at Heidrick & Struggles, especially the concept of specialization on a global scale.

Change wasn't always easy. In fact, a substantial group of senior partners in both companies initially resisted any major changes to their firms. They were proud of the global brands they had created. But major changes were required, and I was the lead executive in both firms to implement the specialization business model to revitalize each firm. And given the fact that I was the first CEO of one of the world's leading executive search firms to be hired by another at that point in the history of the industry, this joint experience helped me discover some crucial secrets.

Here is why this should matter to you. Through personal experience and three decades in the executive search industry, I know what it takes to get promoted. I know what companies are looking for in their leadership candidates. And I know how to get on their radar screen. Today, you might find yourself in one of these three levels:

- *New and unfamiliar* | Maybe you're fresh out of college and new to the world of executive search. But you're a sponge for information and long to be successful.

- *Experienced and open* | Perhaps you're familiar with names like Heidrick & Struggles and Spencer Stuart, but you don't know how to get your name in their databases.

- *Seasoned and successful* | Or you're a seasoned leader and have a great job. Still, you're looking for that next challenge and opportunity to advance your career.

Regardless of which level you find yourself at today, I believe this book will prove useful. As you'll soon discover in the following pages, I've walked through all three levels myself. While my career feels like a trip to Disneyland, I can promise you it didn't start out there. I wasn't born with a silver spoon in my mouth.

My parents were married a combined seven times before I was five years old. I was an only child without any cousins near my age, and I didn't even know what my real name was until I was nine. I've been dyslexic all my life. My grandparents who raised me didn't finish grammar school, and my grades were below average all throughout high school and college.

But in some ways, I think these deficiencies gave me a certain advantage. Because I wasn't the sharpest knife in the drawer, my plan was simple. I would work harder than my competition to go as far as my abilities and energy could possibly take me. Despite graduating from the only college that would accept a 2.8 GPA, I was chosen as the Outstanding Graduate of my class of 2,000. I had at least twenty different jobs or ways of making money before I went to college.

My personal philosophy in business was that no one could outwork two of me. This meant if I worked twice as hard as the average person, everything should turn out all right. Early on, I made several key resolutions. Not only would I have a voracious work ethic, but I was determined to have a happy family and sacrifice whatever it took to make this happen. It's not by chance I've been married to the same woman for nearly sixty years. I wanted to be a role model for my family, colleagues, and friends. I wanted to make things better for as many people as I could by changing whatever I touched.

And another resolution I made to myself? I would travel. Prior to college, I had never ventured outside my home state. But now this would change. I wanted to see as much of the world as possible, work in the biggest and best organizations, and advance to the top leadership roles in all of them.

Yes, I dreamed big. But here is what was amazing: almost every resolution I made came true!

How did this happen? It's a good question, and it'll take the remainder of this book to unpack the details. But I'd say the key was that I had a vision larger than where I was at. I didn't just think about having a *good career*—I thought about having a *good life*.

This is the key. Sometimes in our quest to climb the corporate ladder, we fixate on what will take us to the next rung. But we lose sight of the larger picture and never question if our ladder of success is leaned against the wrong building. We spend our entire lives *climbing* and never *living*. This was a pitfall I resolved to avoid. Yes, I would climb. But I would also live in the process. I would do my best to find convergence between my avocational life and vocational life. I wouldn't just show up for a job. I would do something I loved.

While this book will unpack some of the critical secrets that will help you advance your career, my hope is that it will do more than that. I want to help you rethink the way you define success, to enlarge your dreams, and implant in you a passion to become a change agent.

To many, this type of life feels far beyond their grasp. But I can assure you it's possible. When I look back on my forty-five years in the workforce, I can honestly say there were very few days I *worked*, but there were an incredible number of days I *lived*.

I write this to encourage you. Maybe your life didn't start off on Easy Street. And whenever you walk into a room, you seldom feel like the brightest person around. Gradually, doubt starts to creep in. You wonder, *Can I really make it? Do I have what it takes to be successful? Can I get out of the routine of just showing up for a job, and start really living?*

After eighty-five trips around the sun, I can tell you it is possible. It's not easy. But it's possible. The key word is *change*. And change happens in many different forms.

Unfortunately, when many leaders think of the word "change," they think of words like "strategy," "culture," "process," and "organization." But real change takes place with people. Things don't change. People change.

In my opinion, every leader has only three levers to change behavior. The first is a lever called *harder*. It's utilizing threats or incentives to motivate people do what you want them to do. The next lever is *smarter*. This involves training leaders through seminars and personal coaching to help them excel. But the "golden lever" method of change is what I call *closer together*. It's bringing together avocation and vocation. It's combining what you love most with what you do best. This is where the magic takes place.

Change starts at the top but is driven from the bottom up. It begins with a leader that has a specific vision for their organization and a compass to reach their destination. When you're dealing with the service world, you must first find out what your client wants. One of the ways I did this was with a survey to glean accurate input. I went to the level of the organization where the bulk of the workers would be performing tasks to implement what the client wanted or needed.

From here, I sold this idea to management and communicated this change repeatedly. This meant everyone had ownership of the change and was recognized for their contributions. And the more I could recognize and reward them financially for their contributions, the better. While people naturally resist change, I've found that when they are part of and can tangibly benefit from the change, they take pride in their work and develop a sense of ownership. Any time you create a winning environment, everyone's career is enhanced by being a part of a superior business model and can claim part of its victory and success.

If you're reading this book, chances are you are or want to be a leader. But to be a great leader, you need to be a great change agent. If the whole concept of change doesn't sound pleasant, you're not alone. Few people like change. And often, pain is the only incentive that brings real change. But if you want to be successful, fulfill your dreams, and live a great life, there are ten changes you need to make. The first one starts with you.

CHAPTER 1

CHANGE YOURSELF

I f personal upbringing is a predictor of success, I was doomed from the start.

To say I grew up in a dysfunctional home would be an understatement. My biological father walked out on me the night I was born. The night my mom gave birth to me on July 30, 1939, in Solano County Hospital in Fairfield, California, my father's girlfriend came to the hospital to borrow fifty dollars from my mom so she and my father could get married. Crazy, I know.

Not surprisingly, this marriage didn't last long. Dad was an alcoholic and ended up on skid row as part of the Sacramento homeless community. Being homeless wasn't a new concept in my family because my grandmother was also homeless for most of her early life until she married my Papa Joe at fifteen. Dysfunction was everywhere, and there was so much I didn't understand. Living in a home situation that was less than ideal, I spent much of my time playing referee between my mother who wanted to visit and my grandmother who didn't want her around.

Because my parents didn't take responsibility for me during my developmental years, this meant I lived with grandparents on my mother's side from day one. My Papa Joe was my idol. He was a jack-of-all-trades and master of many. He was captain of the fire department, police commissioner, town band leader, a builder, eventual mayor, and one of the most generous people I've ever known.

Ron's grandfather, Joseph Gerevas, who raised him until he was a teenager

Born the son of Portuguese immigrants, Papa Joe started with nothing. His parents were sheep shearers, and every month was a struggle to survive. But years of eighteen-hour workdays later, Papa Joe's efforts paid off. By the mid-1920s, his hometown of Fairfield, California had a population of eight hundred residents, which was about 1 percent of its size today. Over a few years, Papa Joe's real estate portfolio grew to include the town theatre, clothing store, ice cream parlor, food market, restaurant, pool hall, and bar.

Then the Great Depression hit, and money dried up. People couldn't buy groceries, and they certainly didn't have funds to play pool. Rather than leverage his position of power and become a town dictator, Papa Joe decided to help others in need. He relinquished his assets and forgave townsfolk debt—keeping only a small sporting goods store he'd run for the next twenty years. That was the kind of man he was.

There was nothing he couldn't do. Papa Joe taught me invaluable life lessons, such as "Leadership starts by being a good role model," "Actions speak louder than words," and "Happiness starts at home." He taught me that everything has great value and that going into debt was never good.

Papa Joe was the ultimate change agent and a stickler for doing business the right way. I still remember him driving back to a supermarket to confront a salesclerk who overcharged him by $1.23. While the cost of the gas likely exceeded the amount he'd earn on his refund, to him it was all about principle. Merchants should be honest with their customers.

I remember him telling me that he thought the town needed a marching band for their holiday parades. He'd never played any instrument before, but that didn't stop him, and within a few years he played almost every instrument and became the leader of the Fairfield band.

Papa Joe taught me anything was possible, and everything I know about leadership today started with him.

COMFORTABLE ALONE

Raised as an only child by my grandparents until I was a teenager, I had no one in my immediate family less than a generation older than me. The only people who came to our home were grown-ups. Because our home was small, I wasn't allowed to have friends over to play. Keeping in mind this was well before the age of iPhones, computers, and electronic games, one might wonder what on earth I did to pass the time. My grandfather didn't even own a television and refused to purchase one until I turned ten.

I spent every holiday with adults and never had a birthday party at my house with friends. I was also very small. Despite constant ear and throat infections, my grandmother refused to have my tonsils removed. As a result, my doctor said this impacted my natural growth. It also meant I spent a lot of time sick and out of school.

Ron at ten years old

I was the shortest and smallest boy when I entered high school at 5'3, 103 pounds. I was always the last person picked when we formed teams to play sports in our neighborhood. On those rare occasions I hung out with kids at the beach, I was the kid they picked on. But as soon as I moved to my mother's house at thirteen, I had my tonsils removed, and this helped my growth. I became the center and the highest scorer on our high school's junior varsity team at five feet, eight inches tall. A little more growth helped me earn ten trophies in ten different sports through college.

I was an introvert who received energy from studying my inner thoughts and ideas. I was perfectly comfortable playing games by myself and against myself. Whenever I lost (which was every time), I analyzed my mistakes and thought about what I could do differently to beat myself the next time. While most kids learned to play tennis by playing against a friend or adult, I learned to play by hitting balls against a wall. Since the wall never missed a return, it became my strongest competitor. Eventually, I hit enough balls to become the only freshman in my high school to earn a varsity letter and make the freshman team at my college that won the NCAA National Championship.

These combined experiences meant I spent endless hours sitting, thinking, and playing by myself. I thought about who I was, what I wanted to become, and how I was different from my friends. What I thought about most was why certain things happened to me and not others. What could I have done differently to achieve a different outcome? I can't tell you how many times I thought to myself, *Remember what you just did or said and make sure you do better next time.*

But in an odd way, my unconventional upbringing worked to my advantage. While some today might label my childhood experiences traumatic, I can honestly say there was never a day I felt unloved. Yes, I had obstacles. But there were so many good moments. I had people who cared for me and loved me. Most important, I refused to dwell on any disadvantages I had and was comfortable in my shoes.

Getting to know myself was one of the best steps of childhood development I was ever forced to take. Most people aren't comfortable to sit alone with their thoughts. They always need something to distract them. But I felt that getting to know myself was key to my early development and gave me a head start in my professional endeavors.

Questions about personal identity that many adults only confront in their thirties were ones I was comfortable addressing in my teens. And while there might have been times I "grew up too fast," I can now see how my unusual upbringing worked to my advantage.

This growth in self-awareness proved useful in my career.

SELF-AWARENESS IS A JOURNEY

If Aristotle was right when he said "knowing yourself is the beginning of all wisdom," I would add that being true to yourself is the first step toward building a successful career.

The whole concept of self-awareness has become the buzzword in management over the past few decades. When I first started my career in the 1960s, terms like "emotional intelligence" and "self-awareness" were nonexistent. Workers showed up to do the bidding of their bosses. But looking back, I realize I was talking about these concepts long before they were popular. Self-awareness wasn't a catchphrase for me. It shaped the way I thought. It changed the way I behaved.

While most people *think* they are self-aware, few *are*.

No one achieves full self-awareness. We all possess blind spots. But the key is to do all we can to limit our deficiencies. I'm convinced this has been one of the primary reasons for my success. Because I knew myself well, I was able to effectively navigate life's challenges.

The sooner you know who you are, the better your life will be. And the better you know yourself, the higher your chance of fulfilling your dreams. Knowing yourself helps you navigate between right and wrong decisions and have proper expectations. You know what you can and cannot handle.

This pursuit of self-understanding is a never-ending journey. Because with each stage of life, fresh understanding emerges. You learn more about who you are as your needs change. And the older you get, the more your behaviors and beliefs change. And if your expectations don't shift along with these changes, you're in trouble.

When you know yourself, it's easier to understand why you can make better decisions that impact your life.

For example, it's difficult for most to know when the time is right to change jobs and pursue a new opportunity. Transitions like these normally create a lot of stress and second-guessing, which often leads to an uncomfortable case of buyer's remorse. However, if you are in tune with your core beliefs and values, your self-awareness will give you enough self-confidence to make the right decision and be excited about your new challenge.

START WITH THE END IN MIND

Sometimes it's best to live life in reverse and start with the end in mind.

An effective way to do this is to write out your retirement speech now. Ask yourself, *What else do I want to accomplish in my career before I retire?* Visualize yourself standing before a crowd of coworkers at your retirement celebration and think of those things you'd like to be able to share.

Another powerful exercise you can do is take some time for self-reflection. Ask yourself, *What do I want out of life?* Swiss psychiatrist Carl Jung defined an introvert as a person who received energy from studying their inner thoughts, ideas, memories, and feelings.[1]

---

1   Michelle Badillo, "Theories of Personality: Carl Jung—Analytical Psychology," University of Buffalo, accessed September 19, 2023, https://sites.google.com/site/ubmichellebadillo/theories-of-personality/carl-jung-analytical-psychology.

Assuming this is true, one might define me as an introverted Energizer Bunny. My mind is so active some days I feel as if it is a mini–nuclear reactor!

Another great question to ask yourself is, *Am I proud of the life I'm living?* If the answer is no, you owe it to yourself to change. Being true to yourself means you take responsibility for your actions. You must be honest with yourself.

DEVELOP A PERSONALITY PROFILE

One of the best ways to know yourself is to take a series of personality tests and note the obvious correlations and comparisons.

While one test can be helpful, on its own it gives you an incomplete picture. It's only as you put everything together that things start to make sense. Each personality assessment is like adding one more piece of the puzzle. After taking three or four, the picture becomes clearer.

Three of my favorite tests are Career Leader, Career Success Map Questionnaire, and the Myers-Briggs Type Indicator. When I sit with a person and look at their results on these three tests, I have a good idea of which career path they should choose. While I never tell others what to do, I do prompt them with questions. For example, if someone comes to me with a finance background and wants to know what they should do next, these personality tests give me better insight. If this person is risk averse and doesn't like change, I'm going to steer them away from Wall Street and into something with more stability, such as government or education.

Personality tests help you know yourself. And after you're done, it's helpful to run your findings by a friend to see if your profile matches their perspective of you.

YOU ARE RESPONSIBLE

Everyone has an idea for how you should live. Advertisers want you to buy their products, bosses want you to behave a certain way, and family members have their own set of expectations. If you're not a secure person, you will be pulled in a thousand different directions.

But the *only* person who has your full best interest in mind is you.

In the past, companies felt a responsibility to help *you* grow so that in turn *they* would grow. Your success was linked to their success. This meant you didn't have to worry about your future because you knew your company always had your back. They took responsibility to ensure you were taken care of and climbed the corporate ladder in the proper manner and at the right pace. If you were loyal to the company, worked hard, and fulfilled the company's expectations, you could expect to enjoy a fulfilling career and not have to worry about finding another job.

But this world has largely disappeared. Gone are the days where you remain with one company for forty-five years and they make sure you're trained, promoted, and compensated and receive a gold watch for your efforts. Instead, those early in their careers today can expect to have over a dozen jobs. Many will have a lot more. According to the Bureau of Labor Statistics, "The median number of years that wage and salary workers had been with their current employer was 4.1 years in January 2022."[2]

As Reid Hoffman and Ben Casnocha describe it in *The Startup of You*, "We are all self-employed today—there is no job security. We're living in the age of downsizing, right sizing, freelance consultants

---

2   US Bureau of Labor Statistics, "Tenure and Occupational Mobility among U.S. Workers: Technical Note," accessed September 19, 2023, https://www.bls.gov/news.release/pdf/tenure.pdf.

and self-employed workers."[3] Yes, there are still some of those well-established, leading organizations that still exist and do everything they can to retain employees for as long as possible. But they are the exceptions. Due to the increased costs in goods, services, and staff, most of corporate America have been forced to cut back on operating expenses to compete. In essence, they have been forced to do what's best for the company while the employee is forced to do what is best for them.

Today, hiring is not the problem—retention is. This simply means workers must learn how to become their own CEO and VP of marketing. Doing what is best for you means developing the necessary career development skills that I now teach. It doesn't mean you're unprofessional or act to the detriment of your employer. But it does mean your career development is *your* responsibility.

While this might appear frightening, it is empowering. Just think about how important job searching, interviewing, and networking skills are today. If you end up working in fifteen different jobs, you could easily interview at sixty companies, generating on average four interviews per company—thus totaling over 240 interviews. If this is the case, you had better learn how to do a professional interview and see yourself as others do.

Everything is on you. You are the one who must decide the right time to leave your job for the next opportunity. You are the one to make sure you find fulfillment and satisfaction in your job. You are responsible for creating positive change, learning as much as possible, and leaving your place of employment better than when you started.

---

3   Reid Hoffman and Ben Casnocha, *The Startup of You: Adapt, Take Risks, Grow Your Network, and Transform Your Career* (Sydney: Currency, 2012).

DEVELOP A STRONG WORK ETHIC

In the following chapters, I'll outline specific changes you can make that will improve your life and the lives of those you lead. But trying to effect external change without internal change is like trying to drive a car across the country without any fuel. Remember, it takes a changing life to change a life.

If I were to look back on my life, I'd say one of my greatest differentiators was my relentless work ethic. I wasn't going to passively wait for opportunities to come to me. Instead, I created opportunities. Case in point, I started my first job when I was just nine years old. Because I lived in a small town, we only had one newspaper, the *Solano Republican*. It was only eight to ten pages and sold for ten cents a copy in small metal stands on street corners. One day, I walked into the newspaper office and asked if they'd give me a stack of papers so I could sell them to people walking the streets, shopping in stores, or eating in restaurants. They agreed and offered me three cents for every paper I sold.

I earned my first dollar that day.

My next job was a major step up the corporate ladder and involved killing flies in all the stores along our town's main street. Store owners agreed to pay me five cents for every fly I killed, a near 50 percent increase in commission. The large thirty-by-seventy-two-inch storefront windows were perfect, especially during the winter and fall months when the warm sun attracted flies like a magnet. By the time I'd turned ten, I was making as much as three dollars a day, and it was time to take my next major step.

I talked my grandfather into letting me cut some small pine trees around our cabin in the Sierras and bring them to his sporting goods store in the back of our truck. I then sold these as Christmas trees in front of his store for two dollars each and started raking in the cash.

When I wasn't selling trees, I was trimming down the local squirrel and woodpecker populations that were wreaking havoc on our cabin. Hour after hour I'd sit with my dog, often killing three to four of these creatures and earning myself a handsome seventy-five cents in the process.

Speaking of hunting, most of my childhood meals came from something our family had either killed or caught. We hunted and fished every season. And because my grandfather owned a sporting goods store, I received all my ammunition free of charge. I caught my first trout at age five and killed my first deer at thirteen. I tracked deer and bear throughout the Sierra Mountains and even won a trophy in trap and skeet at thirteen. And this was likely the reason I'd go on to win a sharpshooter medal during my time in the US Army. Living off the land was how I was raised to live.

For the next four years, I worked in the fruit orchards all summer for ten hours a day, six days a week, serving in multiple jobs such as fruit cutter, box boy, picker, and truck driver. By fourteen, I was free-lancing wherever I could make a buck. I mowed and watered lawns, washed cars, painted buildings, waited tables, washed dishes, made boxes in a packing shed, and pumped gas.

By sixteen, I was making real money with jobs such as carpenter's apprentice, pouring cement, digging foundation trenches, parking cars, pick and shovel yard work, and jackhammer apprentice. During college, I added a few more occupations that included dorm proctor, fraternity president, and singer in a quartet.

While there didn't appear to be a golden thread that connected all these jobs together, I can now look back and see how each one changed me for the better. They helped me see what I liked and didn't like. Also, they highlighted areas I needed to improve and helped me understand how people wanted to be treated.

CHANGING AND BEING CHANGED

Even at a young age, I was a change agent. To me, the principle was simple: *change myself and change others for the better.* Change and be changed.

This soon became a game for me. With every job I took, however menial the task, I did whatever I could to complete it in the most efficient manner possible.

For example, even my nine-year-old mind knew there was a reason many adults didn't buy newspapers. They were either too busy or too lazy to find a stand. But if I could bring the paper to them, then I was in business. It didn't cost them any extra, and it taught me invaluable lessons about the service business.

Flies were a serious menace to restaurants and grocery stores. When I eliminated them, I played a small part in changing things for the better. And by picking the hottest points in the day, I could maximize the number of flies I killed. The same principles applied to selling Christmas trees. Because there weren't many places that sold them, especially at my price, I had a competitive advantage and offered a service people wanted.

Similarly, I spent my time in the fruit orchards finding more efficient ways of doing manual labor. As I stepped into more of a leadership role, I helped redefine workers' roles so everyone knew what they were doing. I eliminated duplication, simplified tasks, exceeded expectations, and celebrated with my team when we all earned more money in the process. In short, the fun of achievement meant more to me than earning a few extra bucks. I was changing things for the better and thus improving people's lives.

Working so many different jobs taught me the importance of adapting. A great example of this was the time I signed up to work a jackhammer on a construction site. At just sixteen, I weighed a grand total of 135 pounds—a mere forty pounds heavier than the jackhammer itself. My crew was tasked with putting in a new sewage system, but there was just one problem. The line for this new system ran straight down the center of dozens of streets covered with four inches of black asphalt—which turned into a tar-like substance on those days that exceeded one hundred degrees. Twice I ended up in the back of a pickup truck wrapped up in blankets, freezing on my way to the hospital from heat exhaustion.

The ninety-five pounds of iron were dead weight and difficult to drag, let alone lift. When you started drilling, if you didn't lift the jackhammer out quick enough, the asphalt would instantly swallow up the blade and require two or three guys to break it free. During my first two weeks, this happened dozens of times. I averaged only two blocks a week and experienced enough muscle soreness to last a lifetime.

But then my mind started to work. *How could I change my strategy to be more effective?* I learned that the secret was to work in sync with the jackhammer. Rather than fight this ninety-five-pound gorilla, I tamed it by levering its power and turning it into a glorified pogo stick. Using this new method, my production skyrocketed. In the next two weeks, I was able to do four blocks a week, and my teeth finally stopped chattering. By week five, I was doing six blocks per week without any stops or mistakes and using half the energy.

KEYS TO CHANGING YOURSELF

Most people like the thought of changing others. Few enjoy the prospect of changing themselves. If you're an introvert like me, you might struggle to think if you'll ever reach your full potential. Maybe you struggle with self-doubt and worry if you'll ever be good enough. If that's the case, know you're in good company. For example, because

I'm dyslexic, I struggle to read. In fact, I'm almost embarrassed to admit this, but I've never read a book from cover to cover—which I suppose doesn't make me the most likely candidate to write one!

But I was determined to make the most out of the cards I was dealt. And instead of reading books, I learned to read people. Instead of focusing on my insecurities, I chose to leverage them to my advantage. I used my learning disability to become a communicator that people like me could understand.

When it comes to our lives and careers, we're all given a certain number of cards to play. Some have a stronger hand than others. Looking at the hand I was dealt, some might look on and say I should have folded. But I never felt that way. And because I didn't have a limiting mindset, I far exceeded what I even dreamed possible.

For years I've followed my own *Field of Dreams* maxim that says, "If you change, they will come." I realized early on in life that bosses and customers had one thing in common: they wanted things changed for the better. If I could find a way to offer a service more efficiently and at a better value, they were interested.

That said, I recognized that changing the world started with myself. To do this, I had to first stop thinking of having a job and start thinking about building a career. I wasn't just working for someone. I was contributing to projects greater than myself.

If you feel you've been dealt a bad hand, do something to change your seat at the table. Don't settle for a phrase like, "I guess everyone else gets all the luck." Be positive. Be present for others. Grow in self-awareness. Always seek to do the next right thing.

Changing the world is great, but changing yourself is where it all starts.

CHAPTER 2

CHANGE YOUR HORIZONS

G rowing up in a small town without any brothers or sisters, I was comfortable being alone and didn't see any reason this should change.

My plans shifted in 1957 when I left home and started my first semester at San José State University (SJS). At first, my plan was to keep to myself, attend classes, and graduate in as short a time as possible. But my perspective changed the day I joined a fraternity.

I didn't want to join, but my boarding house roommate in my first semester at college thought it would be a great idea. He started attending Rush Week, which is the time fraternity members put their best foot forward to recruit new members. And one night he convinced me to join him at a beer party for a fraternity called Theta Chi. He was thinking about becoming a member and figured he'd rope me into the process.

Reluctantly, I tagged along even though joining an organization was not high on my list. To my pleasant surprise, when we arrived, I saw one of my college tennis teammates who was a brother in the house. The evening went well, but I still wasn't convinced. However, the brothers talked me into coming back for one more event.

The next evening, I arrived at the fraternity to hear loud music and more than a hundred brothers and girls gathered outside the red four-story Victorian gingerbread fraternity house. A new powder-blue 1957 Chevy convertible with the top down was parked in the middle of the front lawn. Sitting in the front seat was the Theta Chi Dream Girl, and sitting in the back was her gorgeous, blond sorority sister, who, as it turned out, was my blind date for the evening.

She motioned for me to join her, and together we rode around the neighborhood, circling the twenty-six fraternities and sororities in the area. By the end of this evening, I was sold. I still wasn't a fan of organizations, but if this was what life in a fraternity looked like, you could count me in. Here I was, just a small-town guy who barely knew anyone, and yet I was riding around in a convertible with two of the most beautiful women I'd ever seen.

Today, as someone who has spent thirty years in the executive search industry, I can say with great authority the Theta Chi fraternity brothers put on a master class in recruitment. Their plan of action was simple, realistic, well thought out, and executed beautifully (in more ways than one).

There was just one problem.

Theta Chi fraternity house at San José State University

PLEDGE HAZING

While life in the fraternity house *became* great, it didn't start off that way.

The first three months were downright dreadful. Like all pledges who hadn't yet been initiated into the fraternity, I was forced to endure an entire semester of hazing. At one point, I had to wear a gunny sack for underwear that stretched from my neck to my groin and was every bit as uncomfortable as you'd imagine. I spent a week sleeping on a cement floor, tossing and turning into the wee hours of the morning.

Keep in mind this was 1957, just three years before the federal government passed antihazing regulations. Hazing was in its heyday and, by all objective standards, out of control. In the semester I was initiated, four pledges across the US died. One young man was forced to eat raw liver and choked to death. Another two were tied to abandoned railroad tracks that turned out to be not abandoned, and one drowned in a lake.

Hazing was brutal, and the brothers forced us to do every disgusting thing you might imagine. There were paddling sessions where brothers tried to break a three-foot wooden paddle over our butts. Every Monday night after chapter meetings, the brothers would put us through a new stage of harassment.

The culmination of pledge hazing was Hell Week, a term I'd learn was an accurate description. It was our final test of humility, and many of us would have left the fraternity if we knew what lay in store. The most memorable point of this week was "pledge chow." This was when all the pledges were forced to kneel around a table with hands behind backs and eat the nastiest food imaginable.

THE WILD DAYS

After pledging, life was good.

I was twenty, and life in the fraternity house consisted of drinking beer, dating, partying, playing sports, studying, and enjoying life to the fullest. Sometimes I look back on life in my fraternity and shake my head at some of the wild scenes I witnessed.

For example, this one time I was dancing in a small bar in Newport Beach. It was during one of our college spring break parties, and by noon everyone was hammered. I was dancing next to a group of guys playing darts, and the next thing I knew, one of the darts whizzed by my ear, piercing one of my buddies in the neck. Today, the music would stop, a group would huddle, and someone would call 911.

But these were different days. With zero emotion, my buddy calmly lifted his hand to his neck, removed the dart, threw it at the board, and resumed dancing. Then there were moments I'm embarrassed to admit. One of them was when I got pulled over for drunk driving on my way to a frat party. Dressed in a full cowboy outfit that included a holster, two cap guns, and a ten-gallon hat, I was a bizarre and sorry sight. Taking one look at me and noticing my slurred speech, the officer asked me to step out of the vehicle while he issued a sobriety test.

"Hold your arms straight in the air, close your eyes, and stand on the balls of your feet," he said.

Doing my best to comply, I slowly raised my arms and shut my eyes. But as soon as I tried to stand on the balls of my feet, I toppled over into the officer's arms.

That's when one of my buddies jumped out of the car and said, "I haven't had a drop to drink, and we are less than a mile from the party. If I drive us there and home, would that be OK?" The officer nodded, and we were on our way.

Thank God times have changed.

Another morning when I was president of the fraternity, I woke in our frat house to the sound of laughter. Rubbing the sleep from my eyes, I looked out the window and saw this beautiful six-foot statue of Venus de Milo in the middle of our volleyball court. *I wonder how that got there*, I thought. Before I could say a word to anyone, one of the brothers yelled, "Ron, someone wants to talk to you on the phone, and he isn't in a good mood." The man on the other end of the line was the owner of a prominent Palo Alto restaurant.

"Hello," I mumbled.

"Young man," the owner said, "I'm giving you three hours to return our statue, or you and some of your friends are going to jail." I'd never put two and two together faster in all my life.

"Yes, sir," I said. And thirty minutes later, his statue was back in its rightful place.

There were so many other crazy moments.

A HAMMER, FOOD FIGHTS, AND PAUL BUNYAN

During my years at San José State, we won multiple NCAA titles in numerous sports, and we dominated track and field competitions—producing a high number of US Olympians in the process. In fact, my roommate, Ed Burke, was on our hammer-throwing team and participated in three different Olympics, including the 1984 Los Angeles Olympics when he led the USA team by carrying the American flag into the stadium.

One semester, soon after Ed was just learning how to throw the hammer, we decided to put it to good use. We were in the process of moving out of our one-hundred-year-old fraternity house so we could build a new one. And that's when Ed came home one night after a keg party and decided he'd get the demolitions started with a little hammer practice.

With all the grace of a wrecking ball, Ed went to work. He attached his twenty-five-pound hammer to a long chain and started throwing it through every wall in sight. Up and down the fraternity house he roamed, slamming his hammer into the walls of our front room, dining room, and hallway—giving no thought to the 1:00 a.m. time frame or the twenty guys sleeping in their beds. It was a crazy scene. Our dog was barking, and every brother in the house thought we were being invaded. This escapade proved there was more than one way to get hammered in a fraternity.

If the hammer didn't do enough damage to satisfy the brotherhood, what happened a few nights later should have. We were enjoying a lovely dinner in our large dining room with thirty of us present at three long tables. It was spaghetti-and-meatballs night with a nice tomato, lettuce, and cucumber salad and rolls. As we began, I noticed it was quieter than usual. I soon discovered why.

Minutes after taking my first bite, I noticed a roll fly across the room. Within seconds a meatball took flight in the opposite direction. Just as I started to stand up and put an end to it, the entire room yelled, "Food fight!" and everything dissolved into chaos.

Each fraternity brother grabbed whatever was closest to them and let it fly. Ten minutes later, everything and everyone was covered with food. Spaghetti, meatballs, and sauce were plastered on our faces, hair, and clothes and on the windows and ten-foot ceiling. Lettuce and tomatoes were all over the walls, gallons of milk had been poured on everyone, and broken plates and bowls were everywhere. It took a garden hose, two shovels, and a garbage can to clean up the mess.

Just another day in the life of a fraternity.

THE VALUE OF BROTHERHOOD

I share these stories to illustrate the path to success often begins with a series of false starts. If you were to take one look at the Ron Gerevas who was drunk and partying like there was no tomorrow, you might not have thought there was much leadership potential. But in retrospect, I've realized some of my wild moments at San José State were all about finding my way.

After living a quiet upbringing, the wild culture of life in a fraternity took my world and shook it upside down. And while there were days I didn't handle this change well, joining a fraternity was one of the best decisions I ever made. It broadened my horizons and introduced me to a whole new world.

On one hand, I hated some aspects, such as hazing. And in a few years when I became president of the fraternity, I was happy to bring this practice to an end. Still, in an odd way, I wouldn't trade my experiences for anything. These brothers were not my biological kin, but they felt every bit as close as I imagined real brothers would.

Brotherhood taught me the value of responsibility and teamwork. It showed me the only way to live up to my full potential was to be in close connection with others. If I kept to myself, I'd stunt my growth. But if I broadened my circle of friends, my potential was limitless.

Life during my college years gave me so many wonderful experiences. Despite my added workload, I kept up my mother's wish to take care of my body. My main sport was college tennis, but I was also very active in our intramural fraternity leagues, playing each year on our football, basketball, baseball, volleyball, and bowling teams.

Ron (left) singing with the "Shiloh Four" quartet in 1960

I also continued my grandfather's desires by singing and playing guitar in our fraternity quartet called "The Shiloh Four." We played at all kinds of events, including weddings, pinning ceremonies, dances, hootenannies, and school musical events. While I didn't see it at the time, my years at Theta Chi fraternity and San José State put me on a path to leadership because they showed me how important it was to think beyond myself.

MY FIRST TASTE OF LEADERSHIP

As an introvert, I'd have to say I stumbled my way into leadership. Aside from sports, I refused to let anyone nominate me for any leadership position in high school or college and was content to not belong to anything. Then everything changed. My fraternity decided that for recruiting purposes we needed to have some campus leaders and class officers.

Everyone told me to put my name on the list, but I refused. However, my roommate, the same guy who was my roommate at the boarding house, secretly placed my name on the ballot for sophomore class VP—only telling me he'd done this *after* the deed was committed. When I told him I had no interest and asked him to remove my name, he explained there were five others in the running. These other students were better known, and he assured me there was no chance I'd win.

So I left my name on the list but did zero campaigning. As fate would have it, all five of my opponents dropped out or were eliminated, and I won without ever casting a vote for myself. At first, I was frustrated, but I soon warmed up to life as a leader, and over the next three years, I served as vice president of the Student Body, president of my class, president of the Student Council, president of my fraternity, president of the Honor Society, justice on the Student Court, chair of the Student Union Planning Committee, Theta Chi Social chairman, Theta Chi Rush chairman, and Interfraternity Council rep. While all this extra work meant I had to graduate in five years instead of four, it proved well worth the experience.

MY LEADERSHIP LAB

The college and its extracurricular activities served as my leadership lab. And by leadership lab, I mean that I learned how to run meetings, manage people, give speeches, make decisions, play politics, debate issues, create plans, manage budgets, and motivate groups. This taught me the fine art of being an effective change agent of others. I changed political campaigning on campus by introducing the concept of a party slate of candidates when I ran for Student Body president. I also identified specific candidates for the top five positions in the student body and listed us as the paper ballot with me as president.

Another positive change I made was to improve the way we ran our fraternity meetings. When I first became president, I knew that our current meeting structure was unproductive and inefficient. It wasn't hard to understand why. Trying to run a meeting with forty or more brothers, many of whom had been drinking, was a daunting challenge. But I felt that if I could make these meetings shorter, more productive, more relevant, and more fun, things would improve.

This was when I introduced myself to *Robert's Rules of Order*. Interestingly, I was not aware other fraternities were already using this as their parliamentary guidebook. It was a new concept for us. Combining what I learned in those pages and adding my own improvisions, I came up with my own "Ronald's Rules of Order" and changed the way everything was run. It wasn't perfect, but our meetings now had structure. Little did I know that meetings would become my professional sporting arena and pay major dividends throughout my career.

Along the way, I even picked up a few honors. At the annual senior honors banquet, the dean congratulated me on achieving "The Triple Crown" by being named "Outstanding Graduate," recipient of the Meritorious Service Award and the Outstanding Student Body Contribution Award. These awards helped me attain national recognition by being listed in the Who's Who Among Students in American Universities and Colleges program for two consecutive years.

The SJS administration credited me with establishing the SJS Judiciary Disciplinary System as a liaison between the student body and the school's administration. This gave our students more say in student disciplinary matters, and this change was seen as a major victory for our students.

The other day I was going through one of my old scrapbooks and came across this note from the national Theta Chi president. He wrote about my role in helping our fraternity get a new house and said these words: "As Chapter President, Ron played an instrumental role in securing the largest loan ever given by the National Board of Trustees for a new chapter house." I'm sure that was one of the reasons I received first runner-up honors for the Colley Award, which is the annual honor given to the "Outstanding Theta Chi in the Nation."

Our new house changed our lives immediately. It would have never happened except for our dedicated alumni.

KEYS TO CHANGING YOUR HORIZONS

As you can see, life at college and in my fraternity was a roller-coaster experience. There were days I hated and days I loved. Saying goodbye to the comforts of home and embracing new surroundings weren't easy. There were moments I was homesick and longed for those quiet times of hunting alone in nature. But I have no doubt these decisions compounded and set me up for later success.

Sometimes it's only as we're stretched out of our comfort zones that we see what we're made of, and our true personalities come alive.

Taking the path of least resistance is easy. However, if you find yourself faced with the choice between broadening your horizons or playing it safe, I'd challenge you to take the first option. Go to a school where you don't know more than two people, start a job that feels a bit over your head, and tackle a challenge that gives you butterflies.

Steps like these help you change your horizons.

CHAPTER 3

CHANGE YOUR FOCUS

After each spring semester of school was over and my "leadership lab" closed for the summer, I used my time to travel across the USA, fulfill my military obligation, experience life as a union worker, and meet world leaders, national politicians, and top entertainment performers.

That's a *lot* to unpack, but let me give it a go.

My first two summers during college were mundane. I joined a union and spent them as a carpenter's apprentice and foundation laborer. For three months, I put my muscles to work and helped build track homes in my hometown of Fairfield, California. My girlfriend's father was the big boss, and this came with its share of perks.

Life as a foundation laborer was not quite so glamorous. Each day, I stood in a trench behind the blades of a large ditch hole digger, a bandana tied to my head, and ear plugs jammed in as far as I could push. Temperatures hovered around 100–115 degrees, and I must have drunk a good three gallons of water every day. As the machine did its work, I followed behind with a shovel in hand and cleaned out any of the loose dirt that fell back into the trench.

The dust was so thick I couldn't see the digger ten feet in front of me. Every thirty minutes we'd stop, and I'd unscrew the lid off the canteen of water strapped to my waist and clean the mud pies that had formed around my eyes.

Despite the solid pay and benefits, I soon realized this life was not for me. I enjoyed hard labor, but added responsibilities like ditch hole digging, cement mixing, and jackhammering convinced me the hard labor route was not going to be my destiny.

As it turned out, my summers were about to dramatically change.

LIFE AT BOHEMIAN GROVE

In the summer of 1960, I'd just turned twenty and was heading into my junior year at San José State University when I started work at one of the most exclusive men's organizations in the world—the Bohemian Club. Located in San Francisco with a membership wait list that exceeded twenty-five years, the Bohemian Club was my introduction into a world I'd never seen and didn't know existed.

For two weeks in July, my fraternity roommate (whose relative was an influential judge in San Francisco) worked as part of the camp crew. Using his inside connections, he got me a similar job. To this day the Bohemian Club owns an exclusive 2,700-acre campground in Monte Rio, California, called Bohemian Grove. This is a five-square-mile area within a redwood forest that the Russian River runs through. It is made up of 130 small encampments with tents erected on wooden platforms. Each encampment has about ten to thirty members who have their own help to take care of everything they need (except for camp-wide entertainment and meals).

Every year, hundreds of the most influential male leaders in the world attend this two-week vacation and entertainment summit. Their motto is "Weaving spiders, come not here," meaning you should leave your politics and work at home. The opening ceremony is called the "Cremation of Care," which suggests attendees leave their troubles and problems at home. No cars are allowed in the Grove.

The moment I laid eyes on this place, I was awestruck. Everything was luxurious and over the top. Members and guests would sit on carved-out redwood logs to watch entertainment and eat. And there were three beautiful entertainment theatres among the redwood trees. One was on the side of the hill, another situated around a pond and river, and the last in a beautiful outdoor amphitheater.

Like a scene out of a movie, redwood trees would open ten feet from the ground, and male opera singers sang as their voices carried through the forest. There were dramas, dances, an orchestra, and performances by the best in the business. No women and no TVs or radios were allowed. Only newspapers.

During my two summers, I had the chance to meet Herbert Hoover, Richard Nixon, Tennessee Ernie Ford, Earl Warren, Andy Devine, Henry Ford, and dozens of ambassadors and generals. I remember one evening when I sat on the lawn watching a play with Bing Crosby and Bob Hope just in front of me.

This was my first taste of the world elite, and it was an eye-opener.

My main job was Registrar Captain, and I oversaw signing everyone in and out of the camp. My office was cut into the bottom of an enormous redwood tree. It was an unbelievable setting. More than once, my jaw dropped as I realized who I'd just met. Because there were so many world leaders going in and out of the camp throughout the day, I had to be able to let everyone know where each person was at any given time. Daily calls from members of Congress, celebrities, and different countries were taking place throughout the Grove and my redwood tree station.

My other job at the Grove was Captain of all the automotive placement engineers. At least this was the title I created for the next few years on my résumé. My actual job responsibility? I parked cars. This job was so much fun, and it was always a delightful surprise to see which guests would show up next. *Would it be Art Linkletter or Henry Kissinger?*

One of the ways I earned extra money was by chauffeuring celebrities to the San Francisco airport, which was an hour away. The most interesting passenger was Jimmy Doolittle, our four-star general who received the Medal of Honor for leading the famous "Doolittle Raid" over Japan in WWII. I counted myself among the luckiest men on earth to have him sit next to me in the front seat of my car for over an hour. And I'll never forget my ride with comedian George Gobel in which I laughed the entire way to the airport.

My roles gave me the chance to meet everyone in the camp. Sometimes I loved these interactions, and other times I left disappointed. Most were respectful and went out of their way to be kind. Most treated college students like myself as you might expect accomplished gentlemen to do. A few of the members were downright jerks.

This last group always took me by surprise and left a sour taste in my mouth. I remember thinking to myself, *How can this actor who seems like a kind gentleman in a movie be so condescending?* Secretly, I wished I had some magical ability to take his talent and give it to someone more deserving. One resolution I made to myself was that if I ever became successful, I would always treat others like I wanted to be treated—with respect.

I often wondered if the Grove would become part of my destiny. I knew the management and had met many of the influential members, but I was still doing my undergraduate studies and had just begun to think about my career. And the thought of pursuing membership in a club that would take twenty-five years to join wasn't on my radar screen. Besides, much as I respected most of the members, even this twenty-year-old kid knew this elitist setting was not for him.

THE TRIP ACROSS OUR NATION

After spending two summers at the Grove, I was ready to see the world, or at least more than just the state of California.

As a small-town kid who'd never been out of state, I joined forces with three other fraternity brothers and set out on a three-week sight-seeing bonanza. The reason we used to justify our trip was to attend the annual National Theta Chi Convention in New Jersey. Because there were over 150 fraternity chapters nationally and we considered ourselves one giant family, we were able to hop from house to house on our adventure and experience sights we'd never witnessed. Those were some good days. And the price was right.

On nights we couldn't find a fraternity to take us in, we parked our car next to a city park, unrolled our sleeping bags, and slept under the stars. Some nights were grand, while others were less than wonderful. One morning I woke to shrieks from one of my friends, who was lying ten feet away. I looked up just in time to see two stray dogs using his sleeping bag as their urinal of choice. Then there was that horrible thunderstorm in Utah that forced us to make a beeline for our car. But by the time we all got inside, everything was soaked and we all smelled like wet chickens.

We had so many bizarre experiences. I'll never forget being in Chicago one night and witnessing a stabbing on a small bridge. When the group turned on us and started yelling, we hightailed it out of there and drove to the other side of town. Another morning, we were near Boston at 8:00 a.m. driving on the turnpike through a rainstorm at seventy miles per hour, when one of the guys suddenly yelled, "This is our turnoff!" Our driver panicked and whipped the steering wheel to the right, forcing our car into a slide. Luckily, we didn't flip over, but we did smash through a road sign and slide on the grass for another fifty yards.

Aside from a few scrapes and bruised egos, no one was injured. My car had to be towed, and for the rest of the trip we had to tie one window and door in place. But we didn't care. We were just grateful we were alive and could still drive.

Our final destinations were the Miss America beauty contest and the National Theta Chi Convention, where I received my second-place trophy for Outstanding Theta Chi in the Nation. By the time we finally returned to San José, our spirits were high and worlds enlarged. While some might look at adventures like this as a waste of time, I look back on this summer with great fondness. To me, every moment, whether this be work as a foundational laborer, time spent with the elite of Bohemian Grove, or taking a wild ride across the country, was an opportunity to grow and change myself for the better.

A TIMELY CONVERSATION

If there was a downside to all my extracurricular activities and work in the summer, it was that these made it hard for me to focus on my education. I was so busy doing everything that'd I lost sight of the very reason I'd started school in the first place.

That's when I had a crucial conversation.

Near the end of my junior year, the dean of men, Robert Benz, asked me to stop by his office. I knew Dean Benz because he oversaw many class leadership activities. When I sat down, he said, "Ron, you are about to complete your junior year, and you have yet to declare a major. Don't you think it's about time you make a decision? You are doing a great job as president of your class, but you need to pay more attention to your schoolwork. Let's look at your transcript and talk about some options."

For the next thirty minutes, we had a sobering conversation about what I needed to do to get back on track with my studies. This was my first serious career discussion, and I left Dean Benz's office with a new major and reinvigorated attitude about my education. His timely words were just the spur I needed. While I'm not sure he ever realized the impact he had on my life that day, it was a life-changing experience.

Now that I teach and coach students, I often think back to the instrumental role Dean Benz played in my life. Had he not taken time out of his day to put me on the right path, I might have wandered around for years with zero focus. But that conversation woke me up, and I realized I needed to take my life more seriously.

Partying around and having fun with the guys was great. But if I was going to make something of myself, I needed to know what I wanted and follow that path with passion.

THE CHALLENGE OF FOCUS

Focus isn't easy. Sometimes I look back on my upbringing and think about some of the people who could have done great things but lost track of what was important. And then there were others I knew who lost their focus but got back on track.

Case in point, shortly after my twentieth high school reunion, the FBI contacted me and said they were in hot pursuit of one of my former fraternity brothers. I hadn't spoken to him in years, but he had stolen more than $600,000 from the State of California government and was in deep trouble.

Ironically, my brother's nickname at the fraternity was "Animal," which gives you an idea of how he fit in with the group. When I knew him, he seemed like a honest guy, and I was shocked to hear this allegation. Thankfully, that was not the end of the story. After spending seven years in prison, this brother gave me a call while I was at work. Apparently, he'd been out of jail for over a year and wanted to catch up.

"Hey, Gerevas, what's happening, Bro?" he asked, speaking as though we were still in college together.

"I'm doing well. What's going on with you?" I answered, unsure what to think. I didn't know he had been released from prison. *Did he want money? Did he want a place to stay?*

"Not much," he said. "I'm in town on business. Do you have time for a beer after work?"

I said yes, and as we drank, I found out he was the chief lobbyist for a California association in Sacramento. I couldn't believe his turnaround.

We talked about life in prison, and, knowing the prison he'd went to had a nasty reputation, I asked him, "How did you survive?" I'll never forget his response.

"Ron, I was the only guy with a college degree."

I asked him to explain.

"When I went to prison," he said, "I went to the top gang leader and said I had a college degree in accounting and wanted to be his director of finance. As part of this deal, I did his tax returns and helped him with investment advice." In his words, "If I hadn't pulled that off, I'd be dead."

That was some quick thinking, I thought to myself. But his story just got better. Rather than waste his years behind bars, this brother turned his life around and spent the next seven years developing additional skills to further his career. By the time he got out, he was able to get an even better job than the one he'd had prior to his incarceration.

Lack of focus nearly cost my brother everything, but proper focus got him back on track.

Private Ron Gerevas in the Army National Guard, 1962

JOINING THE MILITARY

Two years after my conversation with Dean Benz, I signed up for the military. The Vietnam War was in full swing during the 1960s, and after receiving my undergrad degree, I joined the Army National Guard with another fraternity brother. For the next six months, I went through basic training and served as a private with the intent to return to San José State and complete my master's degree.

This short tour of active duty took my focus to a new level.

On day one, in our first formation, the sergeant bellowed, "How many of you have a college degree?"

I proudly raised my hand, only to notice I was the *only* one to do so out of 250 guys.

Everyone snickered as the sergeant grinned and said, "Gentlemen, it appears we have someone smart enough to clean our latrines. Young Gerevas just volunteered for latrine duty for the rest of the week." I never raised my hand again.

My time in the military was short, but it was intense. I recall thinking to myself, *At least it can't be worse than the hazing with my fraternity*. But as it turned out, it could.

We ran five miles every morning at 5:00 a.m. along the beach, the cool breeze of the ocean hitting our bare skin. Wearing only a T-shirt and shorts combined with heavy breathing meant almost everyone got sick. In fact, the nickname for Fort Ord in Monterrey, California, was "Fort Pneumonia." Every week we had guys sent to the base hospital, and a couple even died from spinal meningitis. We all had to be quarantined at the base for a couple of weeks because it got so bad.

The positive side was that I loved being fit, and the harsh training environment made me feel as though I was living in a different body. But the downside was there were days I didn't know how some of us survived. We'd go on these long runs, and those who were not in great shape kept falling to the ground from exhaustion. What made matters worse, the entire unit had to go back to wherever that person fell and restart at that point.

At first, everyone yelled nasty verbal comments at the less conditioned guys when they collapsed. But eventually, they realized if they didn't pitch in to do their part to help the weakest finish, we would all be sleeping on the beach instead of in our bunks that night. Everyone learned we were all members of a larger unit that accomplished much more when we worked together as a team.

Thankfully, as it turned out, my education came in handier than it first appeared. Two weeks into my latrine duty, the second officer in command became ill. And guess who the company commander asked to teach his land navigation course? That's right, Mr. College Guy.

The final for this course was beyond description. A couple of weeks prior to the end of basic training, they loaded all 250 of us into several large, closed-canopy trucks in the middle of the night. For the next hour, they drove us all over the Monterrey countryside to only God knows where. When we arrived, they herded us out of the trucks and instructed us to make it back to base by dawn. We had no food and no equipment. Only water. All we had for navigation was a sky full of stars and me.

As the trucks drove off, the weight of responsibility hit me like a load of bricks. It was up to *me* to lead the other 249 men in my company out of our predicament. All we had to do was remember what I had taught them over the past few months.

As the guys stared at me, I gazed at the sky to collect my bearings. In case you don't know, sixty years ago when you were trying to lead a nighttime combat maneuver without any electronic guiding devices, you had to take your lead from the stars. Fortunately, I'd spent a lot of hours doing just this while I taught the class. I found it especially helpful to identify specific constellations and work from there. The more stars I could connect in each constellation, the easier it was to navigate on the ground. Thank goodness I loved my astrology class in college, or we would still be walking.

The officers who dropped us off had been certain to warn us about all the wildlife in these hills, including wild boar and mountain lions. I could tell some of the guys were uneasy. The only weapons we had were knives. That's when my training kicked in, and we started to make our way home, one step at a time. In total, our trip was probably eight miles, but it felt like twice that length given that we didn't know where we were going.

Finally, around 4:00 a.m., we stumbled into camp, tired but ecstatic. The joy of success was wonderful. My guys were giving me high fives and saying things such as, "Ron, you saved our lives!" I must admit it was one of the highest moments of my life.

Life in the military was challenging. Those in my family who served loved it. While my company was on twenty-four-hour alert status to go to Cuba for the Cuban Missile Crisis, President Kennedy resolved this situation, and I never deployed. I finished my basic training in the military just in time to start my master's program in January of 1963 at San José State.

In the military, I met so many different kinds of people from across the country. Prior to enlisting, I had never met a Mormon, and now I knew six. I met guys who came from the middle of nowhere and did not even know what a toothbrush was or how to use it. Four of the recruits thought they had hit the jackpot because they were given army fatigues that had matching tops and bottoms.

Looking back, I can see how my different experiences shaped who I'd become. The fraternity gave me a chance to meet different people from all over California. The military gave me the opportunity to meet people from all over our country. And the Bohemian Grove gave me a chance to meet people from all over the world.

MASTER'S DEGREE AND J. WALTER THOMPSON

After my time in the military, it was back to San José State for my master's degree in business administration.

As soon as I returned, I set up an appointment to meet with my marketing professor, Jack Holland. He was an advisor to one of the fraternities on campus and had an amazing marketing career in New York City. I also knew he'd given some great advice to a few of my friends and was hoping I'd receive the same.

Our meeting was brief but to the point. Jack asked me four clarifying questions. "Ron," he started, "do you want to work in the business sector?"

I nodded.

"OK, which area in business do you think will be the most exciting and rewarding to work in for the next twenty years?"

Pausing for a moment to collect my thoughts, I said, "Marketing."

Like his first question, Jack asked, "What area in marketing do you think will be the most exciting and rewarding to work in for the next twenty years?"

"Advertising," I said.

Jack narrowed his gaze. "In that case, do you know the name of the biggest and best advertising agency in the world?"

I didn't.

"It's J. Walter Thompson," he replied. "They're based out of New York City, and I'm aware of their training program, which is the best in the industry. I recommend they be your target company but realize they are tough to get into because *everyone* wants to join them. They only hire a few inexperienced people each year." There was good reason I hadn't heard about J. Walter Thompson (JWT). Both San José State and J. Walter Thompson were about to celebrate their one-hundredth-year anniversaries. And JWT had only recruited once on our campus in the past century.

As fate would have it, JWT decided to recruit for a second time as I was ending my master's program. As soon as I heard they were coming to recruit, I hurried over to the school's placement office to get on their list for student interviews. Unfortunately, every other student had the same idea, and by the time I made it over, all slots were full and no one else was allowed to sign up.

I was devastated and tried to pull a few strings. But it was hopeless. I even thought about trying to find out which hotel the recruiter was staying at so I could leave him a message. My plan B was to camp out front of the placement office and force him to meet me during one of his breaks. Feeling a bit silly about this idea, I gave up and decided it wasn't meant to be.

The day of the interviews, I'd all but forgotten about J. Walter Thompson and was playing volleyball outside my fraternity house. Suddenly, midgame, one of the brothers yelled from the porch that someone wanted to talk to me on the phone. I yelled back at him to just take a message and that I'd get back with them after the game.

The brother shrugged and said, "OK, but he's at the airport returning to New York and says he is with J. Walter Thompson."

My jaw dropped. *How in the world could this be?* I thought, making a dead sprint to the phone. As it turned out, I had Dean Benz to thank. The J. Walter Thompson recruiter had this habit when he'd visit universities. After interviewing all the candidates, he would ask the dean, "Who is the one student at this university I *didn't* meet today but *should* have?" When this man asked Dean Benz this question, his response was, "You need to talk to Ron Gerevas."

Why? Only Dean Benz can answer. (I'm sure it didn't hurt that I was the Outstanding Graduate of my class.) All I can say is that I'm thankful I took Dean Benz's words seriously. I'm glad I'd made a point of keeping him up to speed on everything I was doing on and off campus. I made sure he remained in my network. And a few months later, I was on a plane to New York City.

KEYS TO CHANGING YOUR FOCUS

In a world of a million options, focus is far from easy. It's natural to chase the latest and greatest adventures. And if you're in your twenties, as I was, there is value in having multiple experiences in different contexts. This points back to broadening your horizons. But at some point, you need to have a Dean Benz conversation and take your career seriously.

The good news is that in today's culture, focus can take you a long way. A recent Gallup workplace survey found only 36 percent of workers were actively engaged in their jobs.[4] It's getting to the place where you're ahead of the game if you just show up. But if you can not only show up but add value to your place of employment each day, there is no limit to what you can accomplish.

---

4   Gallup, "Employee Engagement Holds Steady in the First Half of 2021," accessed September 19, 2023, https://www.gallup.com/workplace/352949/employee-engagement-holds-steady-first-half-2021.aspx.

CHAPTER 4

CHANGE YOUR STANDARDS

Moving to New York City, I felt like I'd landed on Mars.

Aside from a brief tourist visit to New York three years prior, I'd never experienced life in the Big Apple. Everything was new, and I'd be lying if I said my flight across the country didn't include some anxious moments. *Gerevas, what have you gotten yourself into?* I wondered.

Question after question kept running through my head. *Did I make the right decision in moving to New York? Can I compete against the best of the best? Am I smart enough? What will it take for me to be successful? Why did I leave all my friends and family? What will I do if*

I get fired? What will I tell my grandfather and mother? What will I say to Dean Benz?

When these doubts subsided, there was one thing I knew for certain: I'd either succeed in New York or die trying. After attending college, there was no way I was going to slink back to my hometown and tell my Papa Joe I just didn't have what it took to succeed in the real world.

The moment I stepped off the plane, I went into professional career mode. The only person I knew in the entire city was Mike Hooper, the former president of another fraternity at San José State. He was now working at J. Walter Thompson and was there to pick me up as I walked into the JFK terminal. It's a good thing he was, too, because he helped calm my nerves. We also shared similar backgrounds and experiences, and this helped a great deal.

Out of all the changes I'd made in life, this one was the most dramatic. Moving to San José State was a big step, but I was never more than a two-hour drive home. Now, I lived across the country and my safety net was gone.

My first day on the job was one I'll never forget. After walking eight blocks on a muggy July morning, I arrived at 420 Lexington Avenue drenched in sweat. Wiping my face to keep my glasses from sliding down my nose, I got on the elevator and ascended to the twelfth floor. Stepping out of the doors, it was as if I'd stumbled into the world's largest ant colony. Everyone was scurrying about with some important tasks on their minds, and no one acknowledged my existence.

Wearing the only suit I owned, a lovely green, wool one, along with my only pair of dress shoes, my one of two shirts, and one of three ties, I felt more professional than I'd ever felt at any other point in my life. In my mind, I was overdressed for the occasion, but little did I know I'd end up wearing a coat and tie to work every day for the next thirty-five years.

A major reason for joining J. Walter Thompson in their New York headquarters office was to build the best professional brand possible in the field of advertising. Since New York was the capital of the advertising world and JWT was considered the biggest and best firm, I figured that if I succeeded there I could succeed anywhere. There was only one New York City.

FINDING MY COMPETITIVE ADVANTAGE

One of the positive aspects of this move to New York was that my distractions were limited. II seldom dated, hardly drank, and didn't play sports for the first year. As it turned out, I couldn't have afforded to do much anyway. My first "home" was in the Railroad YMCA at five dollars a night. After six months, I graduated to a friend's couch and eventually found a rollout bed.

The YMCA room was just large enough for one single bed, one small chair, and one metal locker for clothes. With roughly five feet between our brick building and the one next door, the view from my two-by-three-foot window was about as grand as the room itself. Everyone in my block of rooms shared a common bathroom, and this created some interesting interactions.

Because the residents of this fine establishment were not exactly posh, I'd jam my bed against the door to keep unwanted intruders at bay. More than once I feared for my safety as drunk neighbors roamed the halls and barged in on unsuspecting tenants.

Working nearly seventy-five hours a week, my life's philosophy soon became that no one could outwork two of me. While most others couldn't wait to party on the weekend, I looked forward to Friday nights because I knew this was when my real competitive advantage kicked in. While my colleagues were relaxing with their families or dating, I had a full weekend to get ahead of them.

As it turned out, I didn't have to wait long before my hard work paid off.

By the end of week six, I was promoted to the new Director of Training position. This placed me in charge of the rest of my training class, which included fifteen others in various departments throughout the New York office. As if this responsibility alone didn't throw me into overdrive, I was also told my first task would be to completely reorganize the entire program—the very training program my marketing professor said was the best in the industry for the past twenty-five years.

During the next twelve months, as I redesigned this program I became in charge of all New York training and orientation programs, which included classes, lecturers, speeches, seminars, presentations, and skills development workshops. The beauty of this assignment meant I was now free to move between departments and interact with the brightest minds in the industry.

By this point, I knew I'd found a home and most of my doubts started to wane. I say *most* because there should always be a little doubt for an introvert such as myself. I compare it to those moments before a competitive sporting event. If I'm not a little nervous, I'm probably not taking it seriously enough or underestimating my opponent.

As the Director of Training, I had meetings with top executives in my building that many of my cohorts had never met. It was a carte blanche opportunity, and I could talk to anyone I wanted, whenever I wanted. Through this unique opportunity, I found ways of getting to most of the decision makers of the firm. I wanted them to see how I ran meetings and made decisions.

In other words, I was marketing myself. And the truth is *everyone needs to be their own marketing director in today's marketplace.*

From nine to five, I bounced between the twelve floors of our building and had one meeting after another with one or more of the twenty-five hundred occupants. In the evening when everyone else went home, I did paperwork until I fell asleep.

DEVELOPING MY PERSONAL BRAND

There were multiple factors that drove my relentless work ethic. A practical one was I much preferred being at the office rather than stuck in my cell-like room at the YMCA. Another was I was overly competitive and scared to death of failure. An even greater reason was I realized this period of my life was a career-defining moment.

I intuitively knew that the first three to five years of a person's career were a lot like childhood. They would forever shape who I would become. Just as a child's brain and personality develop in the first few years of their lives, our brand and professionalism are developed in the first few years of our careers. The more positive our experiences during the early stages of our career, the more options and opportunities we create. At the end of the day, *options* are the key to a successful life.

In the early years of one's career, your corporate personality takes form. How you develop relationships, manage your time, solve problems, sell yourself, and make decisions have all started to take shape. And by now you've made up your mind about how important you think factors such as trust, integrity, fairness, and effective communication are.

I realized that who I'd become was contingent on who I was. And this belief challenged me to change my standards. Dean Benz taught me to change my focus, and now my time in New York taught me to change my standards. Personal brand is important because another word for brand is reputation. Nothing is more important than your professional reputation in the field in which you are a career professional. The quicker you build a successful brand, the quicker you become marketable for bigger opportunities.

Because I attempted to work twice as hard as my competition, my internal brand for JWT was the guy that got things done, changed things for the better, and motivated others. It was this reputation that led to my series of promotions.

THE GOLDEN AGE

When I arrived in New York in the middle of the 1960s, it was the Golden Age of advertising. We were experiencing the dawn of the Creative Revolution, and it was an exciting time to be on Madison Avenue. This was the time when legendary advertising creative director William Bernbach introduced the concept of creative teams.

Two years into my time at JWT, our CEO decided we, too, should be on the cutting edge of our industry. As such, we completely reorganized our entire creative army of 445 staff into a totally integrated, account-assigned creative department. This was a huge risk on his part. We were the largest ad agency in the world and already enjoying considerable success. But our CEO was convinced this new structure would allow us to produce more creative advertising and stay on the cutting edge of the industry.

Ron featured in Bacardi rum advertisement for JWT new business pitch, 1965

Up until this point, all creative personnel in major advertising agencies operated within four separate departments or groups—Copy, Art, TV Production, and Traffic. This made for a long and laborious process. The creation of an ad would start in Copy and receive a headline, theme, concept, or script for the ad. From there, the project went to Art, where members of this team framed the script with the appropriate graphics, visuals, or storyboard format. Next, assuming the ad was meant for television, it went over to TV Production to complete the process. The Traffic department ensured all moving pieces came together in an orderly manner so that deadlines were met, and everyone knew what was where at any given time.

But here is where it got especially complicated. If there was a problem with one of the ads, the entire process started over from the beginning. Sometimes it would take four or five tries to get everything right—which impacted timing, costs, and quality of the product. However, for almost every advertising department in the world, this was a necessary evil they couldn't avoid. That was until William Bernbach came along and introduced the concept of creative teams.

When we introduced this concept at JWT, we took it a step further and integrated all four departments into one called the Creative Department. We aligned all staff into industry and major account specialization teams. Thus, the automotive team was staffed with all creative disciplines responsible for all automotive clients and new business pitches. This meant the entire team was involved at the very beginning of a new advertisement and able to provide essential input that wasn't traditionally captured until a later phase in the departmental process.

To implement this strategy, management established a "Reorganization Task Force." This included the VP of Copy, VP of Art, VP of Traffic, VP of TV Production, VP of Administration, and me. As the Human Resources Director for all creative personnel, everyone involved in this reorganization came under my purview.

This is where my career took an unexpected jump. All five of the departmental VPs had been with JWT since before I was born. But management decided each of them should consult me in regard to staffing decisions. Here I was, a guy who'd been in college less than three years before, now coordinating five men who had a combined 50 years' experience working on one of the largest projects in the firm's one-hundred-year history. Looking back, it's a good thing I never thought about it in these terms, or else I might have caved under the pressure.

Thankfully, this new approach worked, and after one year of operation with this model, JWT increased capacity by 30 percent, achieved a 32 percent higher retention rate, and received 30 percent more creative awards. It wasn't long before the other big agencies followed our lead. For years, JWT had been working harder and smarter. But now, the closer-together change brought all the components together and focused the entire company on the importance of *specialization.*

This new strategy brought together those who preferred working on certain products with those who had the most experience in working on those same products. In summation, it brought together those who *wanted* to be on a particular account team so they could do their best work. The end result was a more creative product.

The analogy I often used to describe why our model made everything so much better pointed me back to my singing days. Before, it was as if each of our four departments were singing a different part—the soprano, bass, tenor, and baritone. In isolation, they were fine. But only by bringing them together did you hear the harmony.

MY GREATEST HIRE

Ten months after my first day at JWT, I made the first and most important hire of my lifetime.

After two quick promotions, I'd quickly changed from being the lowest guy on the totem pole to needing someone else to work for me.

In April of 1965, I hired my first employee who I later promoted and soon after became my bride. She was a sweet, little Italian girl from Brooklyn named Rosalie Theresa Morrongiello.

Ron and Rosalie at JWT when they worked together

Initially, our relationship was strictly business. After my first year at JWT, I started dating another girl for six months and was nearly engaged. But something about the relationship didn't feel right. For starters, she came from an extremely wealthy family. She had so much money that the earnings from her IBM stock alone was greater than my entire annual income! I had never known anyone who had this much wealth. At first, everything was grand, and we got along well, but I soon realized that while wealth was nice, there was something about building a life of my own. I didn't want to *inherit* good fortune.

I wanted to *work* for it and partner with someone who shared my vision.

After this relationship ended, I couldn't help but be attracted to my secretary. Like me, she was getting her first introduction to the big city. While she'd grown up in Brooklyn, New York City was a completely different experience for her. Both of us felt like two tiny ants in a forest of high-rises that stretched to the heavens.

On December 17, 1966, we were married in Brooklyn. And after almost six decades of marriage, I can say one of the reasons our marriage has worked is because we got to know each other in a real and honest setting. We didn't just meet up on dates and start with romantic butterflies. We worked together on complicated projects under stressful situations where we saw each other at our best and worst.

Since she was my first hire, I'd already done my homework. She had to be a good fit because she was going to be my *entire* team. We would have no one but ourselves to lean on for comfort, support, and strength to succeed in this survival arena of the fittest.

Sometimes young people ask me for marriage advice, and if there are any words of wisdom I'd share with someone contemplating marriage, it's to marry someone you would hire. Don't just ask yourself if you feel good being around this person, because feelings can change. Instead, ask yourself if you could work well together.

Today, as I work on this chapter, I can testify this is true. Almost sixty years ago, Rosalie's desk and mine were only eighteen feet apart, separated by a gorgeous, historic wrought iron fence-like structure with glass panes. Now, we share a home office, where for the past twenty years we have shared a built in desk that sits us six feet apart.

NEW YORK STORIES

In addition to finding my life partner, my time in New York served me well in so many ways. It was the perfect convergence of the right time, right place, and right company.

I had so many surreal experiences. One of these was when I'd take the midtown helicopter commuter service from the top of the Pan Am Building (now MetLife Building) to the JFK airport. I felt like I was in a James Bond movie as I flew in between the tall office buildings and saw people in their offices working and waving at me.

Then there were the experiences with famous individuals. At the annual industry-wide 1965 Advertising Association luncheon, I sat next to Lee Iacocca at our JWT table. This was because we were handling over $100 million of Ford advertising, including the introduction of their new mustang model. At the time it was the largest advertising budget in the industry.

Willie Mays was, and still is, my sports hero. One day somebody yelled out to the folks on my floor that Willie Mays was meeting with the president and was just leaving his office. I excused myself from a meeting and ran to the stairwell. I was on the twelfth floor, and the meeting was on the fourteenth. Running down to the fourth floor, I jumped out of the stairwell and pushed the down button on the elevator. From there, the heavens opened. The elevator doors parted, and there was Willie, alone. I couldn't believe it. I stepped in with my hand out and a huge smile on my face.

"Willie, you are my favorite ball player in the whole world," I said.

He smiled, shook my hand, and said, "Thanks, son." I would actually shake his hand again with my son in San Francisco at a luncheon for him.

Then there were my many adventures on the New Haven train. The times I missed my stop because of falling asleep and ended up in Stanford, Connecticut—the final stop on the line—forcing me to catch the next train going back to the city, so I could get home for dinner. The times I would have to stand outside in the snow because all the seats were taken. The time my wife and I went into the city to see a play and a police officer shouted for everyone to get on the floor because of riots in the area.

There was and is no place like New York City, and there was only one Madison Avenue in the world of advertising. In many ways, it was a foreshadowing of my time in government in Washington, DC, several years later. In DC I often knew what the media was going to share before it went public. And in New York, I knew which ads were going to be on every TV in America long before the average citizen. Each was the center of their universe. As such, the intensity level regarding my job created a "live to work" environment rather than a "work to live" environment.

The pace was intense. I always felt I needed to pack my sprinting shoes. In my twenties, this was a good fit. I've always believed there is a time and place for everything. This includes work, and it's why I chose New York to start my career. I was single with no obligations to prevent me from changing my entire focus to a "live to work" mode.

My time in New York City taught me so much.

To prove the power of networking, I was able to get Wayne Nelson, one of my own pledge brothers, hired in the JWT New York office. He's an example of someone who went to New York to earn his stripes on Madison Avenue in advertising and return home to start his own very successful advertising agency—a career path that works well for many.

By the end of my fourth year, I was offered the job of managing our entire Creative Department. But doing so would mean I had to replace someone who had served as the top executive of our creative world for more than ten years and was my mentor and close friend.

At the time, I was twenty-nine and he was fifty-nine. I had been with the agency for four years, and he had been there for thirty-four years. I knew he wanted the role and expected to get it. And after receiving the offer, I knew I couldn't accept it. So I turned it down and requested a transfer to the account side of the business—which is where I had originally been hired to be. Besides, I knew I wanted to return to California in a couple of years and not work on Madison Avenue for the next twenty-five years and become a *Mad Men* character. (Speaking of *Mad Men*, you can imagine how many memories that TV series brought back to Rosalie and me. It took place at about the same time, and other than the excessive drinking and smoking it was spot on.)

By the end of my fifth year, I'd climbed the JWT ladder to such an extent that the JWT chief administrative officer (second-most powerful person in the NYC headquarters office) told me I'd completed the management track of any new college hire by JWT. And he had plans for me to eventually run the NYC office. But three years later, I was ready to return to California and requested a transfer. Initially, he refused. When I threatened to resign, he reluctantly agreed but said, "Mark my words, Ron. You will beg me to return here before long. This city is now in your blood."

But my mind was made up. I loved New York, but if there was any state that was in my blood, it was California. And so, six years after I arrived on the tarmac of the JFK airport, Rosalie and I packed our bags and headed for Los Angeles.

KEYS TO CHANGING YOUR STANDARDS

My time in New York City forced me to change my standards. It helped me understand what it meant to be a professional and gave me the best possible transition out of college.

The problem with many in the workforce today is they haven't outgrown who they were in school. They haven't learned what it means to work hard and become a professional. Maybe they think they know their right career path, but they aren't willing to put in the time. They clock in and clock out. As a result, they never maximize their potential.

If you're in the first few years of your career, I can't stress how important these days are. Each day you show up for work, you're creating your brand or reputation. If you dress sloppy, are careless with the work you turn in, and don't meet deadlines, this stigma carries with you.

This is one of the reasons I encourage new graduates to work for well-known, reputable, branded companies right after graduating. For example, if you want to be an accountant, try to work at one of the regionally or nationally branded accounting firms. It's important to be around others who do business the right way. They're not taking shortcuts and making decisions that if replicated will jeopardize your future in the industry. They teach you the habits of being a successful professional.

Then, after you've learned to do business the right way, if you wish, you can transition to a smaller company and add real value that is based on proper experience or start your own consulting firm now that you are a certified professional and are qualified to do so. There are no shortcuts to becoming a professional. It all starts with raising your standards.

CHAPTER 5

CHANGE YOUR IMPACT

I
f you know anything about twentieth-century American politics, you realize the absolute worst year to start a job in Washington, DC, was 1972. But on August 1, that is precisely what I did. As a *New York Times* article notes, I moved into a building across the street from the White House as Director of Public Affairs for ACTION, the government volunteer agency that included VISTA and the Peace Corps.[5]

As it turned out, this move was only six weeks *after* the June 17, 1972, burglary of the Democratic National Committee headquarters at the Washington, DC, Watergate Office Building. Because several of the White House culprits connected to the Watergate scandal were former J. Walter Thompson employees, this placed me under immediate scrutiny.

---

5   *New York Times*, "JWT and the President," September 24, 1972, https://www.nytimes.com/1972/09/24/archives/jwt-and-the-president.html.

It felt like almost every major executive at the White House had a JWT connection. As the *New York Times* noted, "J. Walter Thompson has been one of the most prolific suppliers of manpower to the Nixon Administration."[6] Bob Haldeman was Nixon's chief of staff, Dwight Chapin was his appointments secretary, and Ken Cole was chair of the Domestic Council. In fact, after leaving New York and moving to the Los Angeles JWT office, I took over for Ron Ziegler, who became Nixon's press secretary. All of them had helped Nixon get elected. I knew most of them and had worked with some at JWT.

If you've ever watched the 1976 movie *All the President's Men*, you saw what felt like home footage of my life. I knew almost all the main characters and lived in that bubble for several years. Sometimes I look back on this era and think about how my life might have turned out very differently had I arrived in Washington, DC, two months prior. Because of my ties to JWT, many in the press would have lumped me in with the same group of people who committed the Watergate crimes.

As it was, the FBI spent months researching my entire life before clearing me to become a presidential appointee two years later. They called my former high school classmates, neighbors, and fraternity brothers from across the country to see if there was anything that didn't add up. Thankfully, everything checked out just fine.

WELCOME TO WASHINGTON

I spent almost five years in DC, and each day felt like I was trying to cram a week of regular job activity into a single twelve-hour span. Day one was no exception.

---

6   Ibid.

Our workday officially started at 9:00 a.m., but on Wednesday, August 1, I arrived an hour early to make sure I was ahead of my staff and able to get a jump on what I expected would be a busy day. When I arrived at my corner office, there was a lone message on my desk with a phone number and the title "Ken Clawson/White House" scribbled above.

Ken was the director of communications in the White House and the most powerful communications executive in the city. He oversaw all communication and public affairs directors working in the federal government departments and agencies, of which I was one. According to Bob Woodward and Carl Bernstein, Clawson was the anonymous author of the infamous "Canuck letter" intended to sabotage the presidential campaign of Edmund Muskie.[7] And in *All the President's Men*, Clawson was the one with the famous line, "I have a wife and a family and a dog and a cat," intended to cover up one of his alleged scandals.

As soon as I dialed the number, I knew something was up because when his secretary came on the line she said, "Ken has been waiting for your call." The way she said it made me realize there was a problem. After a quick "hello," Ken unleashed a barrage of four-letter expletives with my name attached.

It was still fifty-five minutes before I was officially on the clock, and by the way this conversation was going, I doubted I'd be around to even greet my staff.

For what seemed like an eternity, Ken landed one blow after the next, explaining in great detail how I had bad-mouthed the president in a meeting the previous week and expressed opposition to his policies. As soon as I heard that, I waited for the next time he paused

---

7   Carl Bernstein and Bob Woodward, *All the President's Men* (New York: Simon & Schuster, 1974).

to get air and quickly said, "Sir, I wasn't in DC last week. I just arrived yesterday. This is my first day in this job."

After a pause, Ken mumbled, "I think I know what the hell is going on. Keep your head down, your mouth shut, and call me if you need me." With that, he slammed down the phone.

Unbeknownst to me, even though I hardly knew anyone in DC, I'd still managed to create some enemies. Apparently, someone on the Nixon team had been promised my job. And when that person found out he wasn't selected, he set me up to be fired, then left town on vacation for the week. Unfortunately for him, he made one tiny mistake. Originally, I was supposed to start the week before I did. But I delayed my arrival in DC to celebrate my birthday with family in California. Because this rival gentleman had gone on vacation, he didn't know I wasn't around, and thus his setup backfired.

I soon discovered conversations like this were par for the course. In fact, several days later, during my first meeting at the White House with Ken and twenty-five top communications directors in the executive branch, Ken opened our meet-and-greet with this statement: "You all might think that because you are working in a department or agency of our government and have a Secretary or Director that you report to them first. Well, if you do, I've got news for you. Your ass belongs to me." Let's just say Ken Clawson wasn't exactly Mr. Charming.

As soon as I got off my call with Ken, the phone rang.

"Hello?"

"Is this Ron Gerevas?" a pleasant male voice said on the other end of the line. After I said yes, the voice continued. "Welcome to DC. I hope you are enjoying our city. I understand that this is your first day in your new job."

How nice, I thought to myself, *someone from HR is just calling to make sure I'm getting adjusted to the city.* But then the voice continued with this blunt statement: "Mr. Gerevas, I understand you are making $36,000 [which was the highest GS salary level at the time] even though this is your first government position." That got my attention.

"Who am I talking to?" I asked. While my job and salary were public information, it was obvious this was *not* someone from my HR department.

"This is Jack Anderson," the man said. "I appreciate you taking my call. And I wanted to let you know you will be featured in my column this week."

As some readers might recall, Jack Anderson worked at the *Washington Post* and was then the most famous and feared Pulitzer Prize investigative reporter in the country. And on Friday, he was true to his word and included the following write-up:

> Joe Blatchford, the boy wonder who ran the Peace Corps for a while and now heads the new ACTION Agency, has hired a new director of public affairs. He is Ronald Gerevas, who will start his government career earning $36,000 a year.
>
> Blatchford sent around a memorandum announcing Gerevas has been selected "following a six-month nationwide recruitment and talent search."
>
> Presumably, it is just a coincidence that Gerevas hails from the J. Walter Thompson advertising agency in Los Angeles where White House aides H.R. Haldeman and Ron Ziegler formerly worked.[8]

---

8   Jack Anderson, *Washington Post*, August 4, 1972.

I can't help but think that last paragraph contained a bit of cynicism. If I were to guess, I'd say Jack Anderson was trolling for Watergate participants on his "welcome" call to me. He saw the JWT connection and thought he might have found someone who was brought to DC to help his former colleagues.

NOT WHAT I EXPECTED

It's always been my practice to keep my office door open. As soon as I hung up the phone, a young lady appeared at my door and introduced herself as my executive assistant. I couldn't help but notice she was laughing, along with a few others seated just outside.

It was finally 9:00 a.m., and I was officially on the clock. Knowing everyone had observed parts of my two phone conversations, I asked what was so funny. She smiled and said, "Well, it's good news, so l will tell you. We started a pool before your arrival, and based on your first hour, we have already decided you will outlast the three previous directors" (each of whom had only lasted an average of four months).

Before I had time to respond, the phone rang again. This time it was my boss, the director of the agency, and he wanted to see me immediately. As I hurried to the elevator, one of my staff shouted, "You can save time by taking the stairs. Just go through the door outside the office." Stepping out of the office and noticing two doors, I rushed through one, walking straight into a broom closet and hearing a roar of laughter in the process.

Blocking out the pain of my bruised ego, I changed course and headed to the director's office with high expectations. I couldn't wait to engage in meaningful work and do something that would help our five hundred thousand volunteers in sixty-eight countries and all fifty states. After all, this was the only reason I'd taken this job.

However, let's just say my expectations and reality were not in alignment. Without even a "Welcome, glad to have you on the team," the director acted as if I'd been on the job for months and handed me my first assignment.

"Gerevas," he barked, "get me on the cover of a major business magazine as soon as possible."

This wasn't exactly the type of impact I had in mind.

As I soon discovered, this was just the type of person he was. Several weeks later he made an even more flabbergasting request. Hurricane Agnes caused massive flooding in the Pennsylvania area. People were drowning, and homes were being washed away. My director phoned me at 2:00 a.m. to say he needed me at the Andrews Air Force Base first thing in the morning to fly to the flooded area to assess the damage. That part sounded reasonable. But the second part of his request a few hours later wasn't. I arrived at the airport, and as I boarded the plane, my director handed me a can of hairspray. "Ron," he said, "I've got an important job for you today. Stick close to me and make sure my hair looks sharp for every picture."

Such was the mindset of some DC political leaders of that time. In public, they talked a good game about wanting to make an impact. But in private, all they were concerned about was their reputations—especially those with bigger political ambitions. (After the election, a new director took over and things changed for the better. His name was Michael P. Balzano Jr., and he wanted me to help him make major changes throughout the agency. We did just that.)

Next on my schedule was lunch with the director of policy and planning. He had been with the agency for a few months and spent most of his career in education as a political science professor at Georgetown University. As a kind gesture, he wanted to alert me to some of what I could expect to encounter in DC.

He knew I had an undergraduate degree in public administration and wanted to make a difference in the world. After some small talk, he made a government observation I'd never forget.

"Ron," he said, "I spent most of my adult life teaching political science. I have written books and papers on these subjects. But now that I've seen how government really works, I feel I owe all my students and readers an apology. I had no idea what actually happens and how things got done."

Over the next five years, I realized his statement was accurate. If you've never done hand-to-hand combat in the Washington, DC, trenches and are forced to rely on the media and politicians for a true picture of what's going on in this city, you don't have a clue about what really happens.

After lunch, I thought the most eventful parts of my day were over. But when I returned to the office, the director of legislative affairs stopped by to say hello and deliver a new bombshell revelation. He was curious why I decided to join only three months before a presidential election. As he explained, everyone in the current administration at our level would have to submit their resignation to the president just prior to the election.

I explained that I knew there was a risk that President Nixon would lose, but it wasn't likely. (As it turned out, he won forty-nine of fifty states.) The director shook his head and explained that it didn't matter whether Nixon won or lost. *Everyone* would be asked to resign so the president could pick his new team.

I'm not sure why I wasn't aware of this transition protocol, but I wasn't. In any case, when I called my wife that night, I opened with, "We need to rethink our moving date." And we did.

CHANGING THE PEACE CORPS

My initial position as Director of Public Affairs was August of 1972 till September of 1973. This meant I was responsible for all media, advertising, marketing, and public relations. At the time, the Peace Corps was folded into this agency and my only goal in moving to DC was to bring impactful change to this program.

Created in 1961 by President Kennedy, the Peace Corps was a program I'd long admired. It is an international volunteer organization that serves over sixty host countries. Volunteers serve for a two-year period working on locally designed projects. When I was a senior at San José State, I applied to become a volunteer but I never heard back. Hence, when I received a call from a Peace Corps recruiter in 1972 to see if I would be interested in becoming the Director of Public Affairs for the ACTION Agency, I was pleasantly surprised.

Perhaps it would be helpful for me to explain the connection between ACTION and the Peace Corps. ACTION was a federal volunteer agency created on July 1, 1971, by Richard Nixon. When Nixon won in 1968, one of the first things his administration did was consolidate all the federally funded volunteer programs into one agency. This was called ACTION, and the goal was to provide an administrative umbrella for all government-sponsored domestic and international volunteer programs. Domestic operations included Volunteers in Service to America (VISTA), Foster Grandparents, Retired and Senior Volunteer Program, Senior Companions, Service Corps of Retired Executives, and Active Corps of Executives. The Peace Corps was just one of ten volunteer programs under this umbrella agency from 1971 to 1982 (at which point it returned to being a separate agency again).

Because my time in college soured my view on politics, my goal was to quietly sneak into DC and not get mixed up with any of my JWT associates at the White House. I wanted to focus on the Peace Corps, and that was it. But when Jack Anderson featured me in his *Washington Post* section my first week on the job, I immediately received a call from the White House. It was one of my former JWT associates saying, "Gerevas, what the hell are you doing in DC?"

My response was, "I'm here for the Peace Corps, not politics."

Thank goodness that was my response because over the next few years many of my former associates were serving time in prison. What puzzled me was that I knew a couple of them well and would have never imagined this was possible. However, after living and working in the swamp for five years, I saw the negative effects power could have on people. I also saw how the media performs when there's blood in the water.

It's possible I was one of the *least* political presidential appointee that DC has ever seen. In fact, when I first went to DC for interviews, I realized that clearance from the White House was necessary. I had to ask my wife if I was registered as a Democrat or Republican because I didn't know. But what I did know is that the White House was Republican, and if I wasn't registered as one, there was no need to fly to DC. So I went and registered Republican that day, and it worked.

To show how apolitical I was, instead of being sworn in by someone in the White House, I chose to be sworn in as a political appointee at a small ceremony in my office by one of my VISTA volunteers who was an African American woman. I did this so my staff and volunteers could witness and celebrate with me. I doubt if many other DC appointees make that kind of choice.

Ron being sworn in at the White House

CHANGING COMMUNICATIONS

When I started with ACTION, there were two immediate ways I brought change. The first was the launch of a new advertising campaign in 1972. Because it had been twelve years since President Kennedy introduced the Peace Corps to the world, some of the original glow was gone. The Vietnam War had taken a toll on the public, and new volunteer applications were at an all-time low. We needed a new, exciting advertising campaign to revive interest.

The government marketed its programs by using free public service announcements. The challenge was to get TV and radio broadcast managers to play your agency's advertisements instead of thousands of others. We decided to use Johnny Hart's *B.C.* Stone Age comic strip characters, which had been seen by over a hundred million people. We used the tune from "The Alphabet Song" to grab viewers' attention and increase volunteers. I still remember the lines from the times I sang them to members of my staff at agency parties. "A we're the ACTION core. C we contribute more. T is for the teamwork of our crew. I our ideas are high. O oughtn't you apply? N means it's now that we need you. A-C-T-I, we could go on all day. O-N here's why volunteers are needed right away."[9]

Contact your Peace Corps and VISTA representatives:

Peace Corps volunteer recruiting advertisement, 1976

It was simple, but it worked. As a result, we won a CEIO award (Creative Excellence in Advertising) for our efforts. Opinion Research indicated this campaign increased our awareness by 41 percent and Peace Corps applications by 43 percent (ten thousand). In fact, one of

---

9   YouTube, "1974—BC Comic Strip Action PSA," John Hart Studios Inc., https://www.youtube. com/watch?v=Oc9dFe_h7RQ&ab_channel=JohnHartStudiosInc.

my DC highlights was being asked to present our award-winning TV commercial and campaign strategy to all the agency and department communication directors in the city. The request from the White House was to "teach these communicators how to communicate." And the best part was that they asked me to make the presentation in the White House.

CHANGING THE WAY PEOPLE VOLUNTEERED

It's hard to explain the sense of power you feel when you become a presidential appointee in DC and are handed a department, agency, or program to run. There are countless surreal moments. You feel this sense of authority and importance when you testify in front of Congress to get your budget approved for programs that will impact millions of Americans in need. And you feel immense power when you meet with members of the press, knowing that what you say will be read, heard, or viewed by people all over the country.

In September of 1973, I led the merger of all recruitment and communications functions within the agency and became the director of this new entity. This allowed me to completely redesign and implement an entirely new Peace Corps volunteer delivery system, which was recognized by Congress for its improvements. During this time, I traveled to locations including Chile, Guatemala, Panama, the Ivory Coast, Senegal, Malaysia, Thailand, and Uganda.

When I first arrived at ACTION, complaints about unhappy constituents were pouring into my office from Congress. The process for volunteers to engage was too bureaucratic. Volunteers received wrong assignments and were even sometimes sent to the wrong projects.

Host countries complained we sent too many volunteers who had wonderful intentions but not enough skills or experience to make a difference. This led some nations to drop out of the program or reject volunteers because there was not a proper match for them to add value.

This negative feedback prompted us to create an entirely new business model called "Pre-Slot." It took almost a year to create and involved dozens of Peace Corps staff in Washington, DC, and host countries around the world. This new system allowed host countries to request specific types of skills and experience they needed and allowed them to write a job description outlining the specific job responsibilities. Once approved by the Peace Corps country desk in DC, the US recruiting arm recruited someone possessing those specific requirements and tagged that person for the specific job that fit their skills and experience.

It was an instant success, and host countries loved it. I was thrilled to introduce it at our regional Peace Corps Conference in Kuala Lumpur, Malaysia. It reduced the number of days to process and place volunteers from 148 to 79 (45 percent), while reducing our annual operating budget by $500,000. Little did I know how much this experience would help prepare me for the next thirty years of my career in the recruiting industry where I could continue to lead the creation and implementation of new recruitment business models.

THE VALUE OF VOLUNTEERING

These changes I made did not go unnoticed. In fact, the director, Dr. Balzano, publicly stated that "there was no doubt in his mind that Ron was solely responsible for many significant improvements within the agency under difficult, sometimes urgent circumstances." He went on to say that "Ron's performance over the past four years has been outstanding."

I think one of the reasons for this was that my changes not only helped those in need, but they also helped those who volunteered. The new system we established in the Peace Corps was tailor-made for furthering our volunteers' career. This was because we changed the volunteer profile to someone who not only wanted to help others but someone who wanted to serve in a job that required certain skill sets and experiences to be able to contribute.

As a result, volunteers could gain international experience in their field to enhance their careers. Given the circumstances, these individuals would in most cases be given substantially more responsibility than they would have received at home. They not only had a wonderful chance to help others in need, but they could also further their own professional development and résumé.

The lesson here is to consider volunteering to gain specific experience that will help you professionally—especially when you are in-between jobs or can carve out some extra time. You should look for specific charities or community organizations you believe in. For example, if you want to become a CFO, you should look for an organization that needs some financial expertise to help them with their finances, either on a full-time or part-time basis. Experience is experience.

Volunteering is a perfect way to blend avocation with vocation because you are normally not reimbursed for your work and can therefore offer your services for exactly the kind of experience you want to gain. Since you are offering to work without pay, volunteering can also help you explore new areas of opportunity. Incidentally, a stipend was given to Peace Corps volunteers while serving their two years of service because they needed to be able to eat and live while serving thousands of miles away from home.

I served as Director of Domestic Volunteer Programs from April 1975 till December of 1976. This job took me to places from the Arctic Circle to most of our lower forty-eight states. Eventually, I was confirmed by the Senate to lead all US Domestic Volunteer Programs.

President Ford congratulating ACTION Agency for contributions made by agency's older American volunteer programs in 1976

My primary job was to carry out a presidential mandate to increase and expand opportunities for volunteer service in our nation. I was told by the agency director, "Now that you have reorganized everything, run it!" During this time, reporting to the director, I managed a $100 million budget, one thousand staff, and one million volunteers. My mission was to give Americans an opportunity to put their idealism and dedication to constructive use.

CONGRESSIONAL HEARINGS

There seemed to be so many high-pressure situations throughout my time in government. One of these was my Senate confirmation hearing in 1975 to confirm my position as the new Director of Domestic Volunteer Programs.

As you can imagine, there were senators on the other side of the aisle that were not eager to approve another JWT executive into a position of power in the federal government. They made that very clear with their line of questioning. Even more dynamic and circus-like were the appropriations hearings on The Hill. These were times I essentially arm wrestled Congress for approval of my annual budget. To me, these were the ultimate tests in communicating under pressure.

The circus-like aspect was the juggling and rotation of congressional members and their staff during the session. This was caused from some congressional members participating in multiple hearings at the same time. A senator could be gone for twenty-five minutes and suddenly reappear long enough for his staff person to whisper an update in his ear, which quickly generated a question or statement by the senator, and then he was off to another meeting.

If you've ever watched this process unfold on TV, you know it's intense.

In my case, I left the best set of hearings for last. As the person in charge of the agency transition, I initially faced off with six members of each political party with key members of my staff seated directly behind me for any specifics I might need. Members of the media and those in the audience watched as opening comments were made and questions started to flow.

As usual, I thought of this as a "white hat" versus "black hat" debate. The white hats (Republicans) were on my side, and the black hats (Democrats) were on the other. The white hats asked questions that their staff and my staff had worked out prior to the hearing. This was my time to sound brilliant. The black hats asked questions that their staff had prepared for them to either make me look bad, make my request seem excessive, or make a statement they wanted put in the congressional record to make them look good.

DOING GOOD UNDER A CLOUD OF BAD

It's hard to describe this era to people who didn't live through it. On one hand, there was the cloud of the Watergate scandal that engulfed the city. At any moment, I expected *Washington Post* reporters Bob Woodward and Carl Bernstein to show up at my door, demanding I tell them what I knew—which was nothing. And on the other, there was so much progress being made.

Keep in mind our country was in potentially the most turbulent political season of the twentieth century. The Vietnam War, the United States' relationship with China, and the nuclear threat of the USSR made the early days of Watergate a sideshow to the main events.

There are so many stories I could tell.

Because I was committed to building strong relationships with the Senate, I was willing to travel whenever and wherever to help resolve senatorial constituent issues. And one of these trips took me much farther north than I had ever been. There was an important congressman on our appropriations committee who insisted I investigate volunteer complaints from one of our Alaskan projects in the Arctic Circle. Yes, *the* Arctic Circle.

A few weeks later, I took five planes from Washington, DC, to Seattle; Seattle to Juneau; Juneau to Fairbanks; Fairbanks to Kotzebue; and Kotzebue to an Alaskan native village. I made sure I was able to visit volunteers, staff, and community projects throughout the entire trip. The first flight started in a 747, and the last one ended up in a little two-seat piper cub with an Eskimo pilot flying more than two hundred miles about a hundred feet off the ground over nothing but tundra.

We landed near a small stream, where the mayor of the village greeted me. She was a nice woman who took me up the river in a small outboard motorboat to reach her village, which turned out to be a few long streets made up of wooden pallets side by side with a few dozen mud huts on either side. At one end was an enormous pile of broken-down snowmobiles, and on the opposite end were two buildings. One was an all-purpose food and entertainment building and the other for business affairs and a medical clinic.

There were only two VISTA volunteers serving the village, but they were working closely with others in the region. They were convinced the natives in the entire region were suffering from food shortages and unusual health issues. One issue causing some of the problems was a disruption in the migration patterns of the Western Arctic caribou herd. After a full day of meetings, I was convinced they needed help. So, after giving a speech in Fairbanks and meeting Alaskan Governor Jay Hammond in Juneau, I returned to DC and made sure the right agencies were informed to deal with the situation.

Years later, I learned from one of the volunteers that our efforts made a real difference and the situation was improving. They succeeded in discovering new food sources and a creative way of better tracking the caribou herd for the entire region, thereby impacting thousands of Eskimos.

Stories like this kept my engine going. In fact, I needed a trip out of DC every so often to be with volunteers and watch them work their magic. When you work day in and day out in the swamp and deal with bureaucracy for ten to twelve hours a day, you need to recharge your batteries by getting out and seeing the good work being done.

I also made extensive efforts to address the difficulties of Native Americans. I visited eight different tribes, meeting with their chiefs and leaders to evaluate what our volunteers were doing for them and explore what additional resources we could provide. I was so gratified to be able to use whatever influence I had to make things better. My prized gifts were a buffalo bone knife and a very special peace pipe. And my historical moment was having a descendant of the Sioux tribe involved in Custer's last stand give me a personal tour of the battle area.

On Peace Corps trips, I had so many impactful experiences. One of these came during a lunch with the chief of a small hundred-person village in Senegal. The Peace Corps volunteer arranged for me to have lunch with the chief so his people could see how important he was to be meeting with the big chief from Washington, DC.

Ron observing a Peace Corps project in Uganda, 1976

He was an impressive individual who was also the chief mason of the village. We met in his backyard eating area that was a converted chicken coop with wire mesh surrounding us. There were some chickens nearby as well as other animals. The chief, his wife, the volunteer, and I sat on the ground with numerous villagers watching nearby. Our drinks were served in clay cups and had a green milk-like substance (the volunteer described it as koshered yogurt) covered with black horse flies.

Dessert was a slice of melon with so many flies on it you couldn't tell what color the melon was. Since I was the honored guest, my volunteer reminded me I should go first. I quietly asked him how I should bite into it with all the flies. His response was, "Don't worry, by the time it's to your mouth, they will be gone." It was a close call, but he was right. They were wonderful people, and I was proud to make their day.

Then there were the whomp beetles.

When you have twelve thousand volunteers in sixty-eight third-world countries, you can expect some challenging health-related situations. One of these included an infestation of green metallic–colored beetles that sent many of our volunteers and local natives in Sierra Leone to the hospital. When one of these beetles landed on a person's skin, they excreted a fluid that caused an immediate blister. This caused an infection that resulted in serious problems, sometimes death.

Asked by Congress to look into this troubled area, I arrived at the designated campsite just as it was getting dark. The men and volunteers were still out in the fields working, and the women were preparing dinner. We couldn't turn on any lights or start a fire because it would attract beetles.

The locals honored me by giving me the only sleeping arrangement with a roof. It was an old schoolhouse without any windows
or doors. They put a large net over my sleeping bag area to keep the
beetles and other insects and small animals away. Before going to
bed, the volunteer warned me to be careful because there had been an
increase in the beetles, and they were active at night when it was cool.

In the middle of the night, I awoke to noise in the room that
sounded like a small animal crawling around. When it sounded like
this little creature was about to join me in my sleeping bag, I panicked
and turned on my little flashlight next to the net over me. Instantly,
a huge beetle landed within inches of my face on the net. I yelled out
loud enough to wake up half of Africa.

Everyone had a good laugh at breakfast. But I never thought it
was very funny.

A DIFFERENT WORLD

My time in Washington, DC, from 1972 to 1977 felt like a different
world.

I was so naive when I arrived in DC, it was alarming. Although I
had an undergraduate degree in public administration and had held a
few offices in college, I thought I could just show up with my talent,
education, advertising experience, and burning desire to make the
Peace Corps better and it would just happen. If I just continued to
work hard, good fruit would magically sprout. Sometimes it did, but
I totally misjudged what it would take to make a real impact.

I had never been the captain of a ship where I requested the crew
to turn five degrees to the right, only to watch it slowly drift left. I'd
never led an organization where I'd ask a package to be delivered
and discover it had disappeared. And I certainly wasn't accustomed

to making a statement to the media one day only to read a different version printed the next.

There were so many bizarre experiences.

One of these occurred at Dulles Airport in 1975. After boarding a plane one night to give a speech in California the next day, my plane started to taxi out the runway when it suddenly ground to a halt. Multiple securities vehicles with red lights flashing surrounded our plane and made us stop on the runway. Once we did, two uniformed officers boarded the plane and one of them yelled out, "Which one of you is Ron Gerevas?"

I can't remember how many different things were going through my head as I stood up, and the officer came over to me and said, "Would you please come with me, sir?" I thought it was either Watergate related or a family emergency.

I asked the officer in charge what was going on. He replied, "I can't tell you because I don't know. All I know is that it came from the White House."

As it turned out, I didn't have as much reason to be worried as I first feared. The Senate had called for an emergency session and wanted me to testify. As a result, the entire airport was shut down for over an hour, causing multiple delays.

When I returned to the airport the next day for my trip, I got in line for my new ticket. The ticket agent saw my name and turned to all his colleagues behind the desk and yelled, "Hey, everyone, here's the guy who shut us down last night." Most laughed, but I could tell one of them wasn't happy. Ever since that point, I've done my best to never shut down another airport.

Then there was the swamp.

It wasn't until I moved to DC that I realized just how bad it was. Case in point, shortly after I began working in DC, a thirty-five-year-old government employee came to see me. He'd been working with one of our volunteer programs since graduating from college and was now a supervisor. Stepping inside, he got straight down to business.

"Ron, I'm going to shoot straight with you," he said. "I have my own business, and it takes up most of my time. This means I can't work more than one or two days a week, so don't expect to see much of me." He went on to let me know that two of my predecessors had wasted a bucketload of money and time trying to force him to come to the office and work more. Both had failed miserably. And with that, he left my office.

I immediately reached out to HR and our legal team to see if his story was accurate and what we should do about it. Their advice was to leave it alone. They advised that I walk away and focus on the positive things I wanted to do. So I did just that, until this man was caught stealing government funds to payroll his own business. There was no way I could overlook this. It took a lot of time and resources, but we finally got him fired and kicked out of the government.

One less swamp creature. Or so I thought.

Seven years later, after I was back in California, I received a packet in the mail informing me this person had appealed his case multiple times until he found a willing judge to reinstate him back into the agency. This move included a promotion, total back pay, and benefits for the seven years he'd been out of office. Such was life in the swamp, and it's one of the reasons I've declined all invites to ever return to DC.

LIFE AFTER WATERGATE

On the day Richard Nixon resigned (August 8, 1974), the instant political upheaval made it more difficult to function. But after a few weeks, once Nixon and his powerful sidekicks were removed from office, the entire city got back to business as usual, and it became much easier to get things done.

There were sad moments, and then there were happy ones. My wife's favorite evening included a lovely dinner at a Cabinet secretary's home in Georgetown followed by dessert and coffee at the White House with President Ford and the First Lady.

All events at the White House were a special occasion. If only I had a video of the time my wife and I drove our eight-year-old Ford Torino up to the front door of the White House. The back of our car included our son's car seat, along with toys and animal crackers. To make matters worse, the cars before and after us were chauffeured limousines. Thank goodness we were at least dressed properly.

My proclivity for meeting US presidents is interesting. I shook Dwight Eisenhower's hand when I was nine years old as he stopped in our small town on a train campaign tour. I met Richard Nixon and Herbert Hoover at the Bohemian Club. I have two framed thank-you letters on my home office wall from Gerald Ford and Jimmy Carter for working for them. And I turned down an offer to work in the George H. W. Bush White House.

When President Ford lost his bid for reelection, our nine-year-old daughter sent him a letter saying she was sorry he lost and would have to move out of the White House because this meant she would also have to move out of her house. His response I've included in the picture below. My daughter still has that note framed in her house.

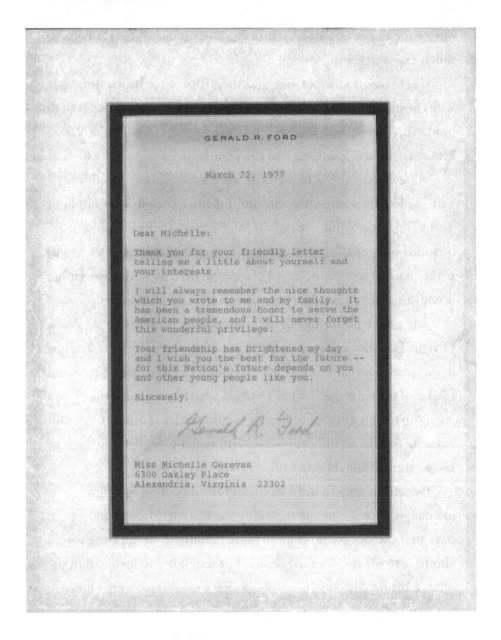

GERALD R. FORD

March 22, 1977

Dear Michelle:

Thank you for your friendly letter telling me a little about yourself and your interests.

I will always remember the nice thoughts which you wrote to me and my family. It has been a tremendous honor to serve the American people, and I will never forget this wonderful privilege.

Your friendship has brightened my day and I wish you the best for the future -- for this Nation's future depends on you and other young people like you.

Sincerely,

Gerald R. Ford

Miss Michelle Gerevas
6300 Oakley Place
Alexandria, Virginia 22302

Thank-you letter from President Ford for serving in his administration in 1977

Before my time in DC ended, I served as the acting director of ACTION from January of 1977 until April of 1977. This meant I was in total charge of the agency's transition to the Carter administration, managing a $200 million budget, two thousand staff, and one million volunteers. My final act in DC was to present President Carter's ACTION budget to Congress for approval.

This process actually started by presenting to President Ford's Office of Management and Budget (OMB) to get approval before he left office. Since it was an unacceptable number to us, we met with President Ford to appeal for a higher number, which we received. But the change in administrations meant I had to present to the new administration's OMB headed by Bert Lance and then again appeal to the new president, Jimmy Carter, to get our desired budget number. Finally, I presented it to Congress and got it approved. Mission accomplished.

KEYS TO CHANGING YOUR IMPACT

My time in DC was the most impactful period of my life. It was truly a mixed bag. On one hand, I witnessed how one could use their power and privilege to abuse others. And on the other, I rubbed shoulders with countless unsung heroes who did their best to make the world a better place.

DC taught me that real impact didn't magically result from having a title. Instead, it came because of everyday men and women who did the unglamorous work others tried to avoid. My time in DC taught me to control my expectations when I was handed abnormal power for a brief amount of time. When I first started, I wanted to change the world. And in some ways, I think I played a part in doing just that. But I also realized that real impact takes time.

Regardless of your position in life, DC taught me there are two primary ways you can make an impact. One is through pursuing power through the path of titles and position. But this often results in disappointment. The other happens through developing the heart of a steward and serving those you lead and help. To be sure, this path is a lot less glamorous. But it helps you sleep well at night, knowing you're living a life of significance.

CHAPTER 6

CHANGE YOUR CAREER

After spending five years in DC, I was anxious to return to the corporate world, but didn't know what I wanted to do for a career. You'd think after over a decade of meaningful success that I'd have some sense of direction, but that was not the case.

As my time in DC ended and I agreed to lead the transition of the ACTION Agency from President Ford to President Carter, I also announced I was returning to California. When I did, that same day my director of training stopped by my office and asked if I'd be interested in meeting with his brother-in-law who was the chairman and CEO of the largest pharmaceuticals distributor in the world. Because this position was in Los Angeles, it sounded like a good fit. Within a month I accepted a position as VP of Communications.

But four months later, about two weeks before I was scheduled to move from DC and start my new career, the CEO called to inform me his board had frozen all hiring indefinitely. This news made me more than a little anxious. At the time, I had an nine-year-old and a six-year-old. We had sold our house and already had all our boxes packed for the big move. Having few options, I negotiated a compensation package that paid for all our moving and living expenses until I found another job in Los Angeles. While the experience was stressful, I've always believed in that old saying, "When God closes a door, He opens a window."

Still not knowing what I would do for work, my family followed through on our plan to move to Los Angeles. At that point, all I knew was that I wanted to change my work philosophy for the next few years from *live to work* to *work to live*. Because I had a young family, I knew that whatever career I chose had to offer flexibility. I wasn't going to miss my son's baseball and soccer games or my daughter's singing and dance performances.

Two months after my closed door, my open window came through an opportunity to enter the world of executive search. I knew nothing about this industry other than it was the gatekeeper to the top executive jobs in the corporate marketplace. After moving to LA, I quickly met with four of the largest and best firms in the industry to land my next position. But instead of referring me to another company, two of the firms asked if I would be interested in joining their organizations.

This caught me by surprise. *What did they know that I didn't?* I knew I didn't want to go back into advertising, but executive search felt like I was stepping into a world I didn't understand.

EXECUTIVE SEARCH EXPLAINED

Before going any further, I should probably explain what executive search is and how it works. Executive search firms specialize in placing high-level executives in both private and public companies. It's their job to assist a company in identifying, evaluating, recruiting, and placing senior management executives. So this is where the action was for creating careers.

There is a major difference between the business models of executive search and traditional recruiting firms. Recruiting firms normally operate a contingent business model. This means they are only paid a fee if they successfully place a candidate. Their searches are usually local and lower management and are seldom done on an exclusive basis.

Executive search firms operate on a *retained* business model, which means they charge an upfront fee paid over the first ninety days of the search whether anyone is hired or not. Historically this fee is one-third of the executive's expected total cash compensation (salary plus bonus) earned during the first twelve months of employment. These searches are normally conducted nationally or internationally, and always on an exclusive basis.

Today, executive search is a $30 billion industry, and there are over five thousand executive search firms. But the top five global firms that do about $8 billion in revenue have consistently been in the top-tier positions throughout the industry's seventy-five-plus years of existence. They are referred to as SHREK and are made up of Spencer Stuart, Heidrick & Struggles, Russell Reynolds, Egon Zehnder, and Korn Ferry. Because of their names and reputations, these firms receive the top searches with the most cache, the most pay, and those searches that define the importance of this service sector.

I started my executive search career with Heidrick & Struggles in June of 1977. While I was new to this space, I thought my transition into this business would be quicker than it was. In fact, my first six months were a disaster. I hadn't completed one search, nor had I generated any new business. What made matters worse, I didn't understand why I was failing.

Then, it dawned on me that for the first time in my career I realized how essential a network was to my professional life. And that old "It's not *what* you know, it's *who* you know" line from my undergrad professor rang true. I'd worked hard to build a strong network in DC and New York, but I didn't have the same connections in Los Angeles.

Having spent the first thirteen years of my career enjoying one success after another, I now faced complete failure. So I did what any reasonable person would do. After seeking advice from my colleagues but experiencing little progress, I made an appointment to meet with my office manager, Hugh Trotter, to resign. I told him I appreciated his faith in me, but I didn't want to embarrass him anymore, and I thought it best to throw in the towel.

Rather than accepting my resignation, Hugh smiled and said, "Ron, give yourself a chance. It's too early to pass judgment. I think you're a great fit for this business."

Because this man was a former McKinsey consultant and a very successful corporate executive, I trusted his advice. *Apparently, he sees something I don't*, I thought. Looking back, I guess he was right, because within a few years, I replaced him as office manager, and a couple years after that I was elected CEO of the entire global partnership.

CHANGE TO QUALITY SERVICE

Of course, that last statement is quite the leap, and some of you might be thinking to yourself, *How in the world did that happen? How did Ron go from giving up on a career in executive search to becoming one of the top leaders in the industry a few years later?* The answer points us back to the importance of change.

After speaking with my office manager, I knew I needed to get serious about this industry if I was going to gain traction. The first step was to gain an accurate understanding of expectations. I realized I was a consultant in a service industry with an organization that was extremely proud of their service to clients. So I decided I had to learn how to serve service-minded groups, one internal and one external. The first were my partners and the second were my clients.

For partners, I tried to put myself in their position and think as they thought. I asked myself, *If I were in their shoes and I was bringing in more work than I could handle, which less experienced consultants would I turn to for help? Who could I trust to do high-quality work and not squander a client relationship?*

The answer was obvious. In 99 percent of cases, it would be the consultant who produced the highest level of quality work. And while quality could be measured in many ways, I saw the quality work my partners valued most was the percentage of assignments completed with a successful placement, or what we referred to as "completion ratio."

This meant that if I became someone the partners trusted, I would hopefully receive the work they wanted to pass off to others. Within the next eighteen months, I focused on quality and achieved the highest completion ratio in our office, and one of the highest firm-wide. In the process, I received as many new assignments from my partners as I generated on my own. Soon, I became one of the highest billers in the firm.

With clients, I adapted a slightly different approach. I tried to place myself in their position and ask a few questions: *How would I want to be served? What deliverables were most important? When would I like to know what? What would be my expectations?* In other words, *How should I serve my clients as I would want to be served?*

The more I focused on quality service to partners and clients, the more my stock in the company rose. Since we were rewarded on an individual performance basis and because I was one of the highest billers in the LA office, I did well financially. While my kids were in school, I rejected any promotions that meant I'd have to work longer hours or travel more days of the year.

But when my oldest entered college, I agreed to become the LA office manager on the condition that I could reorganize the structure and implement a new business model. Our old structure was not working. Our office had lost money for almost an entire decade. In terms of performance, our office was sitting in last place in the United States. My CEO and boss made it clear to me when I accepted the job that I had two years to turn things around. Otherwise, he would turn our office space into a parking lot.

FROM GENERALISTS TO SPECIALISTS

One of the major problems with our Heidrick & Struggles business model at that time was that, aside from our Menlo Park office that specialized in technology, we were almost all generalists.

This was not unusual. Historically, *all* major search firms were structured to serve their clients as generalists rather than specialists. The exception was Korn Ferry that was born out of an accounting firm structure. However, almost everyone in the industry built their practices across every industry to be all things to all people.

To set ourselves apart from the competition, I explored what other more sophisticated professional services industries were doing in specialization. These included such industries as accounting, legal, management consulting, and financial services. As I focused on studying industry leaders, I soon pieced together the best parts of all I had observed. And when my new framework was complete, I launched a new specialization model within our LA office.

At this point, I had a tough decision to make. Should I clean house and bring in a new group of experienced specialized consultants that already had a vision for where I wanted to go and the expertise to make it happen? Or should I stick with the current group of generalists that had been unprofitable for a decade and hope they could adjust to a new style of doing business?

This choice was tough. The LA Heidrick & Struggles consultants were my partners who had served as my mentors. They were my friends, and I had spent time with their families. In a way, it felt a little like my fraternity days. These were my brothers, and they had chosen me to help fix our situation. I felt like I owed it to them to give everyone a chance to change.

The day after I became manager, I took my six generalist partners out to lunch and told them that, starting the next week, our office would be organized into twelve specialty practices. These included six primary groups including healthcare, financial services, technology, professional services, industrial products, and consumer goods as well as six secondary industries. Each consultant would need to choose a primary and secondary industry. Then, I explained that my primary role moving forward would be to help each partner win their competitive shoot-outs so we could collectively drive our overall office revenue growth. To show them I meant what I said regarding team effort, I transferred most of my personal clients to help each partner so that we could get off to a fast start.

To ensure everyone was aligned on the right teams, I hired a Myers-Briggs internationally certified consultant, Dr. Olaf Isaccson, to spend a day with our entire office staff. Everyone took the MBTI self-assessment. This exercise gave me the information we needed to help reorganize and revitalize our new specialty teams. In the words of Jim Collins, it helped me get the right people in the right seats on the bus.[10]

Thankfully, this switch from generalists to specialists paid major dividends. Every consultant exceeded their stretch goals, and within two years we went from being the bottom office to second in performance for the entire country. And within six months after this performance, I was elected CEO with a mandate to continue changing the firm.

Also, for eight years, I served as the firm's marketing instructor at our annual new consultants training program and reorganized it to meet the ever-changing marketplace and increased level of competitive sophistication. Since a significant amount of our new business was generated from winning competitive pitches called "shoot-outs," I felt the need to create an agency marketing manual called "Sure Shots Become Big Shots." This would prove especially useful in the future, especially in my marketing classes.

---

10   Jim Collins, *Good to Great: Why Some Companies Make the Leap and Others Don't* (New York, NY: Harper Business, 2001).

WHEN CHANGE IS TOUGH

In 1980, Heidrick & Struggles transitioned from a founder to part-nership model, and this transition caused significantly more than expected turmoil throughout the firm. We lost more partners in one year than we had the previous eight.

Heidrick & Struggles CEO portrait, 1988

By the time I became CEO in 1987, the firm had lost significant revenue and market share. In fact, *Fortune* magazine published an article on the executive search industry showing we had dropped in total revenue from being number one to number five in the world.[11] This was the wake-up call I needed to convince our senior partners to change. Up until this point, they had refused to believe we had fallen so far that major changes were required. The same article revealed we were closer in comparative billings to number nine than we were to number one. In other words, we were becoming a second-tier firm, and that was unacceptable to everyone.

There have been several pivotal moments in my life that felt like I was the right person at the right place at the right time. This was one of them. Heidrick & Struggles had experienced enough pain to realize they couldn't continue doing what they were doing. They needed someone who was a change agent to step in and rethink the way our business was done.

In August of 1988, one year after becoming CEO, I presented the firm's first three-year strategic plan to the partnership at our annual meeting in La Quinta, California. The firm's strategic planning committee and I had been working on it for a full year, and I'd already worked through some of the concepts in my "Sure Shots Become Big Shots" marketing manual. This plan included all of our internal surveys, paid external research findings, McKinsey consulting input, a new matrixed specialization business model, a new aggressive marketing plan, a revised firm-wide compensation plan, a global expansion plan for new office openings, and a budget analysis and plan to pay for everything. My CFO, Rick Nelson, was instrumental throughout the creation and implementation of this entire plan. His combination of legal and financial expertise was invaluable.

For two days, I stood in the middle of a large room and presented this plan to our entire US partnership and international leadership. I methodically covered every aspect and answered every question and

11   Heidi Fiske, "The Headhunters' Changing Jungle," *Fortune*, 1988.

concern. We continued the process until it was fully understood and approved. As history clearly shows, this was the turning point in our firm. We have never looked back. While it took some of the doubters time to accept our new way of doing business, there is no doubt this new business model made our lives better and more prosperous. Most importantly, it provided our clients with better service.

Looking back our research investment was critical. Why? The Opinion Research findings left us amazed at the differences in what we'd previously *thought* our clients wanted versus what they *actually* wanted. In short, our clients wanted a specialized approach. They wanted someone who knew their business, understood their problems and opportunities, and spoke their language. This further confirmed in my mind that we were headed in the right direction.

Once we had a clear vision in place, it was important to change our compensation program so that it motivated partners to continue doing high-quality work but also meet our new, aggressive growth goals. In the past, we had been paying partners significantly more for successfully completing assignments than for generating new business. I was convinced that we could tweak our formula enough to accomplish both. And so we moved to a more aggressive pay system that paid partners the same amount for handling the business as for bringing in new business. It worked beautifully.

We also incentivized our heavy hitters to generate more business than they could handle by providing them with additional resources to generate more work for others. Because I understood what it felt like to be new to this industry, I realized the only way we were going to grow was if new consultants could initially receive work from more established partners.

In addition, I brought back the Myers-Briggs consultant who had helped me reorganize and revitalize my Los Angeles team and had him work with my senior management staff. At first there was considerable resistance because few people like change. But everyone soon realized why steps like this were important. One of the toughest structural changes was to elevate specialty practice heads to the same level as our office managers. Doing so created an unbelievable leadership matrix that truly made the difference. But it took every political skill I'd learned in DC to pull this off.

The last major change I led was to expand the firm. We did this through adding fourteen new offices on four different continents within the next three years. My San Francisco office manager, Conrad Prusak, played the key role in helping me with this expansion. Asia and Australia were our biggest, but most rewarding, challenges. (We were both grateful for MileagePlus.)

During my first three years, our ranking improved throughout the search world, and the Heidrick & Struggles partnership unanimously reelected me to another three-year term. This was a fabulous period in which we regained our reputation and status in the marketplace.

EXAMPLES OF SEARCHES

Working in the executive search industry was an experience like none other. I'll never forget my first search to find a SVP treasurer for a major construction company. Ever focused on quality, I was determined to complete the search successfully.

After presenting my first panel of three candidates to the retiring treasurer (who was looking for his replacement), he called me to say the leading candidate was a Harvard graduate. There was just one problem. According to my client, Harvard graduates thought the world owed them a living and so they were lazy. Therefore, he wanted me to find another panel of candidates.

I accepted his request, but on our second go-round, things didn't get any better. This time the leading candidate had a mustache, and this outgoing treasurer didn't trust anyone with facial hair.

The third time is a charm, I told myself and felt sure we had the right candidate this time. But once again, there was just one catch. This lead candidate was a Mormon, and as the treasurer informed me, someone who was a Mormon certainly wouldn't be able to fulfill this role because he'd be too busy having and taking care of kids. You couldn't make this stuff up.

Finally, after six months, the VP of HR called and in an apologetic tone said, "Ron, please stop sending candidates for us to interview. It's not your fault. Your choices have been excellent. The CEO forced this treasurer to find his replacement. But he doesn't want to retire, and that's why none of your selections are working out."

Thank goodness I never had another situation like this in my thirty years of executive search.

The good news is almost all my searches worked out. I was only asked to redo one of my placements. After finding the right guy, my placement took another job two months after joining my client's company. I offered to redo the search at no cost. Fortunately, I asked my client if he would like to revisit our number two candidate to see if he was still interested. As it turned out, this selection was a better fit for both parties. Our new placement started on the job thirty days later and remained with the company for over fifteen years.

One of my easiest searches was for the CFO of a fast-growing technology company. I met my client at his office, and, returning to my office soon after, I noticed a new résumé in the middle of my desk. As it turned out, this résumé matched to a T the job description I had just discussed with my client.

Scarcely believing what I saw, I picked up my phone and told my client the story. Because I'd already filled a couple of searches for this individual, I knew he trusted my opinion. While I told him I would continue the search process, I thought we should meet with this surprise candidate because I didn't think he was going to be on the market very long.

The next week, I interviewed the man who had submitted his résumé, conducted a write-up, and presented him to my client the following week. My client hired him on the spot, and to my surprise this placement became a client of mine throughout his entire career and gave me more than five new searches.

My most unusual search completion occurred in 1980 and involved the Getty Museum in Los Angeles. Prior to the creation of this world wonder, J. Paul Getty turned his weekend-vacationing Malibu residence into a small museum in 1954. And I was asked to replace the museum director of what is now called the Getty Villa Museum.

This role involved managing the Getty Villa Museum's $4 million budget and business operations. A year later my placement called me to say he would soon be needing my services again.

"Great, what's happening?" I asked.

"Well, Mr. Getty's estate has just moved $4 billion into his trust for, among other things, the purpose of building one of the finest museums in the entire world (it only required $1.3 billion). This means my budget has just increased from $4 million to $4 billion, so I think I'll need a little help." Talk about an upgrade!

SEEING THE OTHER SIDE OF THE WORLD

While I'd seen much of the world working with the Peace Corps, all those operations were in third-world countries. But opening new offices in countries like Japan, Germany, Australia, Canada, and Sweden in addition to visiting other existing offices in Europe, South America, and Australia allowed me to see a much different side of the world.

I've completed a search in almost every industry that exists. Working out of Los Angeles, I completed dozens of high-level entertainment searches including Lucasfilm, Disney, MCA, 20th Century Fox, and MGM. Where else can you have more fun than working for Skywalker Ranch, Disneyland, Universal Studios, Six Flags, and Knott's Berry Farm? Especially, when you have a chance to work with top entertainment executives like Sandy Climan.

There were so many unique experiences. One of these was working with one of the largest former trading companies in Sweden. They wanted a new president for their US operations. I especially enjoyed having dinner in the CEO's Stockholm residence. Surrounding her twenty-five-foot-long dinner table were photos of at least half of the eighteen Russian czars with members of my client's family together with the czars' signature and personal notes on each.

Then there was my Heidrick & Struggles international president, an ambitious Frenchman whom I loved, even if he spent every day of his life trying to figure out how he could take my job and rule the world. He was exactly what I needed to drive the international side of the business because that was where we needed to expand. We had what we needed domestically to accomplish our mission, but our international footprint was inferior to our major competitors. His hope was that international would eventually swallow up the US.

One of his ways of trying to impress the partnership was by picking a fabulous location when it was his turn to host the firm's annual partnership meeting. His three locations during this period were Paris, Madrid, and London. Paris was majestic, Madrid was eventful, but London was the winner. We stayed at Brocket Hall, which was a few miles outside of London in the country. Built in 1239 and rebuilt a couple of times, it eventually became the hunting lodge for George V and Edward the VII.

This was one of the best times of my life with twenty-eight of my senior partners from around the world serving as the guests of Lord and Lady Brockett for four days at Brockett Hall. They were lovely hosts, and I still recall having dinner one night at their magnificent fifty-foot-long table. I can't do justice, in any description, to the beauty of their manicured landscape that had been used in countless movies. The streams of water flowing all over the property and under six little rock footbridges were sights to behold.

Each of our rooms had a historic English person's name. Mine was King George V's room since I was the CEO. I swear some of the fixtures were original. The bed couldn't have been more than five and a half feet long because I had to sleep crossways to stretch out, and the fixtures and bathtub were barely operational. They purposely wanted you to appreciate the experience in an authentic way. Today it looks like a five-star hotel, completely modernized.

THOSE THAT CHOSE ME

There's a fine line consultants must walk. When a client needs a new leader, they are usually more comfortable if their search consultant has some leadership experience. They want someone with proven credibility and expertise.

This means consultants try to demonstrate their leadership skills throughout the search for the benefit of the client as well as for the candidate. In my case, I obviously wanted to impress the client and develop a long-term relationship for repeat business. But there were a few times I apparently overachieved my goal, and my clients offered *me* the job instead of my candidate.

One of these happened in my second year with the firm. I was invited to join two of the firm's senior partners in a competitive shoot-out for a new president of the National Restaurant Association located in Washington, DC. The team thought I could lend some credibility given my DC experience, and this was a huge search opportunity with one of the biggest associations in the country.

After meeting with the National Restaurant Association board and making our pitch, the chairman turned to my senior partners at the end of the meeting and asked, "Why did you bring along this guy?" Our lead partner responded that while I was new to the firm, my experience in DC might prove useful in this search.

The chairman then looked at me and asked, "Well, young man, what do you think we need, and how would you go about finding that person?"

I gave him my best shot. When I finished, the chairman thanked us for coming and told us the board would decide by the end of the day after meeting with a couple more firms. Later that evening, he called us at our hotel and said, "You have won our search on the condition that Ron conducts the search."

My two senior partners were confused but agreed.

Two months later I personally presented three outstanding candidates and met with the board during the interviews. When we met afterward in a nearby restaurant, the chairman complimented me on the high caliber of my candidates but said they had decided to offer *me* the job.

This was the first time this sort of thing happened to me, and I didn't know what to say. I didn't want to make them mad or lose them as a client. So I said I would certainly consider taking the position if I still lived in DC, but I couldn't uproot my family again so soon. Not used to hearing no, they weren't happy with my answer.

After some back-and-forth, the chairman nodded his head and instructed me to develop a new panel of candidates. This time, they removed the ceiling on compensation and told me to find the best executives possible. I agreed, and two months later I flew back to DC. Once again, we went through the same process but met at a different restaurant.

When dinner was finished, the chairman announced they had made a final decision. He then took his cocktail napkin from under his drink, pushed it over to me, and said, "Please put any number you want on this and be our new president."

Once again, I didn't know what to say. I knew I had to buy time by talking it over with my wife. So I told them I was honored and appreciated their faith in me, but I needed to speak with my wife and children before reaching a decision. My wife and I had gone through this kind of career-changing opportunity dilemma when I turned down previous opportunities in the past, but we now had little ones in school, and so we decided to try it out on the kids.

Several nights later when I was back home in Los Angeles, I presented this option to our eleven-year-old daughter and eight-year-old son while having dinner. When I finished describing the opportunity to our children, my daughter asked, "Daddy, does that mean we have to move back to Washington, DC?" As soon as I said yes, both children screamed, jumped up from the dinner table, ran to their rooms crying, and slammed their doors. I turned to my wife and said, "I guess we're staying in LA."

The next day I called the chairman and gave him the bad news. It didn't go well. He simply asked, "When will you have the next panel ready?" Two months later, we went through the drill again. This time they hired someone, and it was a very successful placement.

There was only one job I'd reconsider taking. In 1989, my former boss at ACTION called to see if I would be interested in becoming the chief of staff for Dan Quayle when he became vice president of the United States. At the time, my former boss's wife was serving as chief of staff for Dan Quayle's wife. This would have been a key leadership role in the White House and for our country.

As someone who had witnessed firsthand how important this position became when Gerald Ford became president, I knew what it would mean to be a heartbeat away from the most powerful nonelected executive role in the White House—maybe the executive branch. I must admit this was very tempting for several obvious reasons. But I was right in the middle of implementing new changes at Heidrick & Struggles and felt obligated to complete our mission.

Given what has been happening to our wonderful country, I'm sorry the White House opportunity didn't occur a few years later. If there's any place on this planet that could use some positive change, it's our federal government.

THE POWER OF NETWORKING

By this point, you might be thinking to yourself, *So what? Why should executive search matter to me and my career?* Here is why.

If you aspire to become a C-suite executive in a Fortune 1,000 company, your name *needs* to be on the radar screens of major executive search firms. Even if you have less ambitious career goals, but you eventually want to earn over $200,000 a year, you need to adopt a strategy to get known by one or more of the five thousand US executive search firms. Doing so should be part of Career Planning 101.

How do you accomplish this? The secret is networking. Because over 80 percent of high-profile jobs are filled through networking, it is critical to make the right connections. In fact, over 80 percent of *all* jobs are the result of networking. When you pursue getting on their radar, here are several points to consider. First, remember that all major search firms are specialized. So go online and learn who the specialty manager is of your desired industry or function. Be creative and find a way of getting your résumé to them.

Of course, if you can have a friend introduce you, this is the best option by far. Finding someone who knows the person is next best. This is where LinkedIn can be especially useful. But in addition to online connections, look for conferences or networking events where you might meet that key person.

In addition, develop your brand. Become a thought leader in your industry and write papers or give lectures. Keep in mind that recruiters don't work for you. They are paid in advance and are obligated to find the very best person they can for the job. Be understanding of their time restrictions and time limitations in getting back to you. Know that they love to receive help in obtaining a prospect or source and won't forget who helped them. And when the opportunity presents itself, they will repay the favor.

In short, engage your networking skills by becoming creative, helpful, and visible. Once you build a relationship with a recruiter, be sure to make them part of your active network. Find reasons to stay in touch. Send holiday cards, send them a message about a favorite sports team victory, play a round of golf together, or grab a coffee when the opportunity permits. Trust me—it will pay off.

KEY WAYS TO CHANGE YOUR CAREER

Over the years, I've had the opportunity to mentor numerous consultants. Some have worked directly for me, and others I've only met along the way. Christos Richards has never worked for me but has remained in touch over the past twenty-five years. He is a good friend, and I helped coach him through three firm changes including compensation packages and employment contracts. Given that he had never made more than $100,000 a year before we met and recently made over $3.5 million says something about the value of having an experienced mentor by your side.

It was also gratifying for me to be able to repay my favorite clients by enhancing their careers. For example, the former CEO of Mattel, Jill Barad, was a terrific client who happened to be the highest-paid female executive in California for good reason. And on my recommendation, she was placed on the Board of Directors for Bank of America.

Regardless of your profession or level of management, make sure that you strategically recruit experienced mentors and coaches into your professional network. It's much easier than you think. Most people enjoy helping others, especially when they are being asked for their advice. They don't expect to be paid, but they do expect to be thanked and shown a little appreciation.

Today, executive search is a little different from when I left the industry fifteen years ago. It has evolved like most other professional services in the marketplace. Technology has led the way for most of the change. AI is already causing the next wave of change. High-potential new leaders have never been easy to find. Well-known, established leaders are known by everybody. Today, the real challenge is *retaining* leaders, not *finding* them.

The real difference is that clients today expect search consultants to be more like management consultants. They expect their consultant to be an expert in their industry with in-depth knowledge of them and their competitors. Of course, this is hardly a surprise to me. Remember, I'm the guy who helped lead the transformation of two of the largest firms into this world of specialization.

At its core, the basics of executive search have never changed. Recruiters are still looking for candidates who are high performers, are strong fits with their new organization, and show the greatest likelihood to remain with them for years to come.

Of course, today's generation thinks a bit differently about their careers than generations of the past. For example, a CNBC article stated that over 70 percent of Gen Z and millennials are thinking about leaving their job within the next twelve months.[12] By contrast, I only worked for five different organizations during my forty-five-year career. When I started a job, I always completed what I was hired to do. When someone put their trust in me to make a contribution, I felt obligated to deliver.

In summary, my time in executive search taught me two things. First, it showed me what was possible if I focused on producing quality service for others. Second, it helped me resolve the question of whether I wanted to *work to live* or *live to work*. I decided neither fit my goals in life and opted for a third alternative—*working to live the way I wanted to live*.

---

12   Morgan Smith, "70% of Gen Z and Millennials Are Considering Leaving Their Jobs Soon," CNBC, January 18, 2023, https://www.cnbc.com/2023/01/18/70percent-of-gen-z-and-millennials-are-considering-leaving-their-jobs-soon.html.

While anyone can and should be happy in whatever home they live, as someone who has lived in a $50,000 home, a $500,000 home, and a $5 million home, I can assure you there is a difference. I knew how I wanted to live and realized I had to change the way I worked to make it happen.

Life is short. Since most of us will spend one-hundred-thousand-plus hours of our lives working, I suggest you take some time to figure out what you love most and do best. Blend them as much as possible. Keep in mind that when you choose a career path, you are often choosing your friends and colleagues for life. So be smart, be persistent, be ambitious, and enjoy the heck out of what God has given you.

In an era when people are changing positions every two to three years, be the exception. This world has a shortage of high-performing, effective leaders. More executives are less engaged in their work today than ever in history. Do what it takes to reach your potential. Become the leader that I know you can be. And how do you become one of those? That's what we'll cover in the next chapter.

CHAPTER 7

CHANGE YOUR INDUSTRY

Change is contagious. And the more you change everything for the better, the more you start to feel invincible. This was certainly my story.

By 1991, I was at the top of my game. Heidrick & Struggles was doing better than ever, and once again we were serving the largest executive search clients in our industry. One of these was for the president of an organization named Jenny Craig—a weight loss and nutrition company. If you're over forty, you might remember them for their 1-800-94-JENNY jingle in the 1990s.

Sid and Jenny Craig were amazing business entrepreneurs, and after launching their Australia-based company in 1983, they took their business to over $400 million in sales. By the early 1990s, they decided to take their company public. Before they did, their securities firm felt they should have a professional manager help them through the public process and then manage their new entity.

After receiving a call from one of my Heidrick & Struggles partners about this search, he suggested I be involved in our competitive pitch when meeting with the Craigs. This was a high-profile search we did not want to lose. So I chose Tom Mitchell, a partner in the LA office who I thought would be a great fit to conduct the search, and together we met with Sid and Jenny Craig at their headquarters in San Diego.

The pitch went well, but there was something strange. As soon as we finished our conversation and stepped into the elevator, Tom turned to me and said, "Gerevas, do you realize we just spent the last two hours listening to them describe *you*?"

I didn't think much about his statement, and my response was, "Great! Since you know me so well, this should help us get the search and make it easy for you to find someone."

But four months passed, and we hadn't heard a word from the Craigs about whether they had decided to use our services. During the interim I was reelected unanimously by the Heidrick & Struggles board to serve as CEO for another three years. As timing would have it, just as we were enjoying some office champagne to celebrate this election, Sid Craig called. He apologized for taking so long to get back with us and said he had finally reached a decision.

"Ron," he said, "if *you* agree to take this job, our search is over."

This felt like déjà vu all over again and took me back to my meetings with the board members of the National Restaurant Association.

A TOUGH CHOICE

"Sid, I'm flattered," I began, "but I can't accept your offer. I've just been reelected CEO of Heidrick & Struggles."

Even as I spoke, I could sense Sid's mood darken. Fearing he was about to hang up on me, I threw out an alternative option. As CEO, I'd always made it a practice to handle a few searches on my own. Since I'd just finished a large project, I said, "Sid, if you want someone like me, who knows me better than me, then let *me* do your search."

His tone changed, and he said he'd think about it. I thought I'd never hear from him again, but to my surprise, two days later Sid called and gave me the green light.

The search started well. Because it was public, I received as many calls *from* candidates as I made *to* them. Every marketplace leader understood this fast-growing $400 million company was planning an IPO. This meant an opportunity to join as president and become CEO of a billion-dollar NYSE San Diego company within a couple of years. Not a hard sell.

Initially, I thought I would complete the search well within the normal three-month search process. But after my first panel of three candidates, I wasn't so sure. Once my candidates were ready, I met with the Craigs at a restaurant. In a moment that felt like I was in *Back to the Future*, Jenny said, "Ron, this was a great panel of candidates. But you promised someone who was like *you*, and none of these candidates are."

After explaining I was still not the person they were looking for, I developed another panel of candidates. This was met with the same result, and it wasn't until eight months into the search and my third panel of candidates that I started to seriously consider this job as a possibility.

One evening, I sat down with my wife, and we discussed the pros and cons. Rosalie didn't want to move because she was very involved in her own business. She was working for Jacki Sorensen's aerobic dancing program as the Los Angeles area manager and oversaw a hundred instructors and five thousand students. Since both children were in college, we had just ourselves to think about when we did our usual pros and cons analysis.

Taking out a legal sheet of paper, we started scribbling down the pros:

- Money and IPO stock.

- A NYSE public company and IPO experience.

- A chance to become CEO of a billion-dollar NYSE public company.

- A chance to make a positive impact on our national obesity crisis.

- As a marathoner, I liked the idea of being involved in the health and fitness industry.

- We wanted to eventually move from Los Angeles and retire in San Diego. Our son was living in San Diego, and our daughter was planning to move there as well.

- Relentless pursuit by the Craigs.

- This would be a new challenge. Besides, I'd already made all the changes at Heidrick & Struggles that I wanted to make.

- A guaranteed three-year contract as a safety net. (Plus, I knew I could always go back to the world of executive search.)

This was quite a list, and the cons were few:

- There was the risk of working for an entrepreneur founder.

- I'd be saying goodbye to a job I loved and a company I respected.

- The timing wasn't great, and two years later would have been more ideal.

In the end, the pros far outweighed the cons, and I took the plunge.

LIFE AT JENNY CRAIG

The first few months at Jenny Craig were better than expected. It was a bit of a commute from LA to San Diego, but the transition was wonderful, the welcome warm, and the environment energizing. In late 1991, we launched a successful IPO and came out at twenty-one dollars a share, steadily moving up in the high thirties to within an inch of a billion-dollar market cap.

Oh, and the amenities were amazing. I could have charged a fee for guests to step foot in my office. It was that spectacular. The Craigs had an architect rebuild a section of their headquarters for the new president, and the final product was stunning. The desk and cabinets were made of rosewood, my conference table was composed of an enormous piece of green marble on a majestic green rug, and the view was spectacular. From the moment I set foot in this space, I knew where I would hold all executive meetings and parties.

Organizationally, I got to work on implementing some basics of professional management. I started chairing weekly executive staff meetings with the top officers in the company, including Sid and Jenny. Some thought this new management practice was a waste of time while others welcomed it with open arms. But once everyone realized these meetings brought value to what we were doing, they were all on board.

This experience further reinforced in my mind how difficult it can be for some to embrace change. It made me think back to my time at Heidrick & Struggles and the day I first introduced my strategic plan. While a few leaders thought it was great, most referred to it as "Ron's damn plan," and only when it demonstrated value did leaders start referring to it as "our plan."

The executive staff at Jenny Craig went through the same cycle. While everyone finally bought into the process, I could sense early on that my position at the company was strictly based on short-term performance. So long as our financial numbers trended in the right direction, everything would be great. But if anything changed and our success waned, I might find myself out of work in a hurry.

THE LAWSUITS

As stock and sales moved upward, I garnered more trust and assumed additional responsibilities. And as I did, Sid spent less and less time with the day-to-day business operations. Instead, he focused his attention on buying a professional sports team, racehorses, and vacation homes.

But that's when everything started to unravel as the weight-loss industry came under attack. As Robert Howe noted in the *Washington Post* in 1993, "19 plaintiffs alleged that Nutrisystem's program caused them to lose weight too rapidly and did not provide sufficient calories or fat to stimulate the gallbladder to release bile to aid in digestion of fat. The results, the suits alleged, was that bile crystallized into painful gallstones, requiring surgery."[13]

Within months hundreds of plaintiffs filed additional class action suits against Nutrisystem. Only a couple were aimed at us, but the collective damage to our industry was devastating. Soon, the Federal

---

13   Robert F. Howe, "Popular Diet Beset by Puzzling Debate," *Washington Post*,
     March 7, 1993, https://www.washingtonpost.com/archive/local/1993/03/07/
     popular-diet-beset-by-puzzling-debate/d26968c7-1b52-43f3-b7bb-331f4466d84d/.

Trade Commission jumped in with their own investigation into the validity of these claims. Too much for the public, it didn't matter that any of the allegations were ever proven true. The damage had already been done.

That said, our real issues at Jenny Craig were not just *external*. There was also too much *internal* resistance to change. And I could understand why. Sid and Jenny Craig had started their company from scratch and built a thriving global business. In an odd way, this confidence became their Achilles' heel.

In *The Innovator's Dilemma*, Clayton Christensen writes about what happens when leaders fail to keep up with the times and adjust to threats. Referring to organizations that failed, he wrote, "One theme common to all of these failures, however, is that the decisions that led to failure were made when the leaders in question were widely regarded as among the best companies in the world."[14] This was the story of Jenny Craig.

At the end of the day, I believed in our product. Yes, we were facing some stiff winds of opposition, but if we made a few changes to our business model, we might survive this tsunami of opposition.

THE NEED TO CHANGE

Around the same time these lawsuits dropped, we were in the early stages of creating a new weight management business model. The operating side of the business was very excited and believed this model could add life to our company. But Sid and Jenny were not convinced and hoped a continuation of the same marketing strategy would save the day.

---

14   Clayton M. Christensen, *The Innovator's Dilemma: When New Technologies Cause Great Firms to Fail* (Brighton, MA: Harvard Business Review Press, 2015), 20.

Like the rest of the industry, we had always used "before and after photos" as our marketing strategy. Sid loved catchy slogans such as "Lose 16 lbs. for $16," or "Get three months free plus free food one day each week." In essence, we used the same methods that had been used for decades. We focused on *micro* changes when we needed to make *macro* adjustments. Changes that didn't just help customers lose a few pounds, but changes that helped them embrace a healthy lifestyle.

Our industry was, and still is, desperate for a new model. But regardless of how much I tried to initiate new changes, the Craigs wouldn't listen. They were kind but had fallen victim to their own success. When I shared my idea of a new strategic plan to give our major shareholders, franchisees, and staff stronger confidence that we were managing the entity professionally, they told me this step was not necessary.

Nevertheless, I felt obligated to do something. I could see the ship was sinking and the barrage of lawsuits meant our industry was under constant assault. Nothing short of radical change would quell the tide.

So I embarked on a new, albeit risky, project. When the Craigs went on their summer vacation to Hawaii, I outlined a new strategy with specific changes I thought our company needed to make. Yes, it would have been easier to keep my mouth shut and go along for the ride, but that wasn't what I was hired to do. I was hired to help the organization become more professional, and I wasn't about to walk away from what I felt was right.

Shortly before Sid's return, I left my presentation on his desk. Weeks went by before he even acknowledged he'd received it. He did so by dropping by my office after work one evening. Our conversation was brief. He said he'd read my proposal, didn't want to talk about it, and wanted me to know he'd hired someone else to take my job. However, he assured me there were no hard feelings and he would honor my three-year contract. On top of this, he even wanted me to be the MC and main speaker to deliver the company's business and future marketing plans at our annual Jenny Craig international conference in two weeks.

I was doubly shocked, but I agreed. Two weeks later, I stood in front of a packed auditorium and spoke about the future of the company to over six hundred company staff, franchisee owners, shareholders, and media—just as I had done the previous year. Aside from Sid and Jenny, no one in the room suspected I would be replaced in two weeks.

While this felt like a crazy way to leave my only unfinished career job, it's not as strange as it sounds. I liked Sid and Jenny, and they liked me. I respected their ability to build a $400 million NYSE company. Jenny was one of the most delightful, talented, inspiring professionals I ever had the pleasure of working with, and Sid and I just didn't see eye to eye. It happens.

In a strange way, my final speech was a chance to say goodbye to a lot of great people. On one hand, I felt the more effective and inspiring my speech was the sweeter my goodbye would be. On the other, there was part of me hoping my strong performance would make people miss me more.

On the day I left Jenny Craig, our stock was trading at fifteen dollars a share. But as word got out that I was gone, the stock plummeted. As Funding Universe noted,

> When Ronald E. Gerevas, chief operating officer and president, departed unexpectedly in November 1993, Jenny Craig stock dropped to $11.75 a share. Gerevas' replacement, Albert J. DiMarco, left after just four months; William R.

Lewis, a former business associate of DiMarco who had just been appointed chief financial officer the month before, left with DiMarco. By this time, confidence in the company was declining, and its stock was trading at about $6.25 per share, less than one-third of its original price.[15]

In short, the market knew this was a sign that nothing at Jenny Craig was going to change. The ironic part was the man who was hired as my replacement was the former CEO of Nutrisystem—the very company responsible for creating our industry's mess. As fate would have it, within just a few days, he stopped showing up for work. When I received updates on these proceedings, I couldn't help but think about what could have been.

LESSONS FROM JENNY CRAIG

It would take another book to unpack all the lessons I learned from my time at Jenny Craig, but a few of them are worth mentioning here.

First, working with founders can be difficult. Sid and Jenny Craig were fine people and had done a marvelous job of taking their company to over $400 million in sales. They had discovered a strategy that worked, and saw no need to change. This was fine when life was good. But when our industry came under attack, they needed to be willing to evolve. While I'd always known working with founders was a risk, I suppose I put too much stock in my own prior success. So far, everything I'd hit was a home run, and I figured I'd just find a way to make it happen. But I was wrong.

Second, money is great, but it isn't everything. This was the first time in my career that I'd chosen a job with money and stock being my

---

15   Funding Universe, "Jenny Craig, Inc. History," accessed September 21, 2023, http://www.fundinguniverse.com/company-histories/jenny-Craig-inc-history/.

top motivators. If I were to offer younger readers a word of caution, I would tell them to be careful using this strategy. I'd tell them to think twice before leaving a job they loved for more money. If it's too good to be true, it probably is.

Third, sometimes wrong turns steer you in the right direction. When I look back on my time at Jenny Craig, I still think of what could have been. *What if the unproven class action lawsuits hadn't brought the industry to its knees? What if the Craigs had been more open to change and we could have tackled the real obesity issues in our nation?* But as my wife likes to say, the Jenny Craig decision was "a mistake that wasn't a mistake."

Moving to San Diego was one of the best decisions we ever made. Little did I know that the day I left Jenny Craig I'd spend the next thirty-plus years in this amazing city. Little did I know that my entire family would remain in this area. And little did I know that I'd develop some of the most rewarding business and personal relationships I'd ever make in my life.

BECOMING A McCOY

Days after leaving Jenny Craig, I saw my name on the front page of the *New York Times*. The article said a certain Ron Gerevas might be returning to the world of executive search. This was news to me because this was not my intention. But as soon as this story got out, some of the major firms reached out to see if I'd have interest in joining them. This felt strange because everyone knew I was a Heidrick & Struggles guy. In fact, during my time with this company, I wouldn't have even contemplated working for a competitor.

Most of the people who reached out were friends of mine in the executive search industry. At first, all I did was listen. The more I did, the more it became clear the only firm I would seriously consider was

Spencer Stuart. They had always been our toughest competitor, and I was curious to discover why they'd had so much success.

In fact, Spencer Stuart was the *only* firm that matched or beat Heidrick & Struggles in the annual top-quality firm industry-wide survey. I took this personally, and when I met with the leadership, I'd say there was this mutual sense of curiosity. The leaders admitted the specialization model I'd implemented at Heidrick & Struggles was effective. To their chagrin, they had recently lost many of their senior partners to Heidrick & Struggles and wanted someone to help them stop the bleeding. And who better than the person who had created the wound in the first place?

They made me a generous offer to join them as vice chairman, president of Global Specialty Practices, and West Coast offices manager. My main mission was to help them design and implement a superior business model to the one we had established at Heidrick & Struggles. It was all a bit surreal, and exciting. I loved the challenge of building something better than what I had already helped build. This would be a first, and it provided just the hook I needed to get me back in the game.

Most change agents I've known suffer from the same disease. Regardless of how successful their changes have been, they are never satisfied. Everything can always be better. And the opportunity at Spencer Stuart felt like a chance to implement those ideas I hadn't had the opportunity to implement at Heidrick & Struggles.

To borrow an American Appalachian analogy, Spencer Stuart and Heidrick & Struggles were a lot like the Hatfields and the McCoys—the two infamous mountaineer families that engaged in a legendary decades-long feud. Unlike this nineteenth-century disagreement, ours never reached the levels of the US Supreme Court. But it did have many tense moments of competing for the top global searches.

This analogy was especially highlighted at my first Spencer Stuart executive staff meeting. When the CEO, Dayton Ogden, introduced me and my mission to the leaders of their firm, you could have heard a pin drop. Although nobody said anything out loud, I could sense what they were thinking. *What the hell is going on? Here is this Hatfield responsible for creating our misery, and now you want us to accept him as an equal member of our McCoy family?*

Other than the CEO and chairman, Tom Neff, few believed I would do anything to harm my former family. To them my presence was a threat, and they viewed me as little more than a spy for the other side. But I saw it differently. I didn't view my presence at Spencer Stuart as being disloyal to Heidrick & Struggles. In my mind, I believed that if we built a superior model at Spencer Stuart, the *entire* industry would prosper.

RAISING THE TIDE FOR ALL BOATS

The challenges at Spencer Stuart were different from those I'd faced at Heidrick & Struggles. Spencer Stuart had never gone through the bloody owners-to-partners transition we'd experienced at Heidrick & Struggles. However, Spencer Stuart was going through its own loss of partners because of the new Heidrick & Struggles business model. Thus, the level of pain for each company was about the same.

That said, the culture at Spencer Stuart was stronger at the time of implementation. This made the challenge of embracing major change more difficult. Both Heidrick & Struggles and Spencer Stuart had senior players that initially wanted no part of any change. Eventually they saw the light. Today they would all admit that specialization was inevitable. But back then, not so much. The level of resistance from some of the best in our profession was unbelievable.

Because the rest of the professional services industry had switched to specialization, I knew it was only a matter of time until the executive search world followed in their steps. The leadership of the largest executive search companies were still in love with what got them to the top. Thus, four of the five major SHREK brands clung to generalization. The only exception was Korn Ferry.

Because Korn Ferry was created from an accounting firm, they embraced the process of specialization straight from their founding in 1969. Despite this innovative approach, I knew our industry needed a new specialization model. How did I know this? Because Korn Ferry hadn't made a noticeable dent in their major competition. In fact, during my first fourteen years at Heidrick & Struggles, I can't recall hiring one Korn Ferry consultant or losing one key team member to their firm.

I knew our industry needed a better specialization model. While at Heidrick & Struggles, I felt it would not only get *us* back on our feet but raise the lake for *all* boats. This was the same approach I carried into my initial conversations with those at Spencer Stuart. At this point in my life, I was thinking less about my *career* and more about making a positive impact in an *industry* I loved.

Because I was navigating in unchartered waters, I knew I needed to learn from the best of the best in the professional services world—those who had been experimenting for decades with specialization. By learning from key executives in the financial services, management consulting, accounting, and legal services industries, I was confident we could cherry-pick the best ideas and build a new model that would change our industry for the better.

So I reached out to the guru of professional services, Harvard Business School professor David Maister. Until his retirement in 2009, Maister was widely acknowledged as one of the world's leading authorities on the management of professional services firms. He had written dozens of books on this subject, and *Managing the Professional Service Firm* became my road map. I even had him spend a day with my senior staff at Heidrick & Struggles to share his thoughts on our mission.

Now, it's here I should pause and say I've never been against business competition. Far from it. But after experiencing some success in one's career, I believe there should be a pivot. After you reach your goals and achieve the income you desire, it's time to think beyond your *career* and consider your *industry*.

When I arrived at Spencer Stuart, my days of warring against the competition were over. I had no interest in bringing Heidrick & Struggles down. My belief was that as we switched to specialization, we would increase the size of the pie for all players in the executive search industry.

THE SECOND TIME IS STILL A CHARM

During my third year with the McCoys, it was obvious I was making a difference. Spencer Stuart stopped losing partners, and our winning percentage of competitive shoot-outs increased. Other than a few expected turf battles between the geographic office managers and specialty practice heads, these changes took place without too much fuss. Some parts went much smoother than my implementation of changes at Heidrick & Struggles.

Implementing "Ron's damn plan" a second time was easier than it had been the first. I'd already worked out what did and didn't work. Most importantly, my presence alone at Spencer Stuart meant there was little doubt that the model I'd helped create at Heidrick & Struggles was successful. This didn't mean everyone agreed or was open to change, but everyone knew they had to change *something*.

From day one, I realized my new specialization plan would face stiff resistance. The partners at Spencer Stuart were proud of what they'd accomplished and the strong culture they'd created. And while I had immense respect for this organization, especially Tom Neff and Dayton Ogden, I also knew change was imminent. So my first order of business was to spend time with the most respected authenticators of the culture to make sure they were on board. If I didn't have the trust of senior leaders, I was sunk before I ever began.

This was where my time in Washington, DC, proved useful. Being a Republican in Democrat territory helped me understand how to lead a bunch of Hatfields when I was a former McCoy. To implement the changes I saw necessary, it was imperative I treat everyone with respect. Because almost everyone at the firm either had an advanced degree or spoke more than one language, it goes without saying that I was working among intelligent people. And as a life lesson, when you start messing around with the way intelligent people make a great living, you had better have your act together.

As I mentioned before, it's critical to put yourself in the seat of others during this process and be sensitive to how *much* you change and how *fast* you change it. You also need to clearly communicate throughout the entire process and solicit input on a regular basis. As I did this, I noticed measurable improvement.

MENTORING MY SON

One of the highlights of my career was having my son work for me at Spencer Stuart. Stephen had just received his MBA, and I talked him into working for me for a year before accepting another job. For someone who had spent most of his life trying to help others be successful in their careers, this was a dream come true.

Stephen joined as a full staff member and was treated as a full staff member. His primary responsibility was doing potential candidate research and development. He also participated in new business and marketing projects, and I had the pleasure of introducing him to every phase of the business. He sat in on all our staff meetings, and I had him put on headphones and listen in on me conducting business, negotiating compensation packages, interviewing candidates, and selling our services.

This was postgraduate, on-the-job training where he was totally submerged in professional corporate life. The experience was so wonderful that in some ways I felt *that I* should be paying for our learning experience rather than both of us being paid to live it.

The lesson for you, the reader? If you ever get the opportunity to work with and mentor someone in your family, take it!

A RETURN TO THE McCOYS

After four years at Spencer Stuart, Heidrick & Struggles reached out to see if I'd have interest in coming back. After my departure, they had gone public and were rolling in cash. Knowing I had helped make that possible, I think they thought it was time for me to return to the McCoy ranch. Helping their major competitor no longer made sense, and I agreed.

The timing was good because I'd finished what I said I would do. It took four years to install a full range of global specialty practices and rebuild the West Coast operations to the desired level of operation. I also knew the senior management of Spencer Stuart felt all expectations had been met or exceeded. It didn't come as a surprise to Spencer Stuart that I was returning to Heidrick & Struggles. At the end of the day, they were just pleased I had helped recreate a level playing field for the two firms to compete. The new specialization model was working, and both companies were headed in the right direction.

What made the Heidrick & Struggles offer especially tempting was their willingness to allow me to open a San Diego office. After four years of commuting to the Spencer Stuart office in Los Angeles, this was a welcome opportunity. As an added bonus, I was able to create my own team and work with staff members I'd known for years (the five-year employment contract was a lovely cherry on top).

My five-year contract would take me to age sixty-five, and by then I could get started on the next phase of my life. After forty years of wearing a suit and being on someone's payroll, I was anxious to find some new mountains to climb, take in some new scenery, and decide how I would share with others what I had learned.

Opening the new San Diego office was an amazing experience. Because we were the only SHREK brand in the region, this gave us a big advantage. And none of the major firms set up shop in the market until we arrived.

My two key team members, Pepper de Callier and Elaine Koutris, joined me in San Diego. Because major changes weren't required, it felt unusual. Building a new regional office had its challenges but didn't require ten-hour days. As our five-year contract expired, the firm decided to close most of their smaller offices around the world, including ours. But they asked me to continue working with the firm out of my home. Because this was during the time when much of our industry began to embrace remote work, this proved timely.

During these last ten years with Heidrick & Struggles, my primary client was Sempra Energy, and I became their primary search consultant. I personally conducted more than twenty-five top-level search assignments during this decade. I took great pride in knowing I was the primary conduit through which their new top leadership team was being built. My first placement, Neal Schmale, signaled the caliber of executive I would be introducing as he eventually became president and COO.

When I turned seventy, after forty-five years of being on a payroll every single day, I finally said enough was enough and cut the cord. It was a fabulous forty-five years, but I was excited for a new chapter.

KEYS TO CHANGING YOUR INDUSTRY

My time at Jenny Craig and Spencer Stuart taught me some invaluable lessons about changing one's industry. And if you are in the services industry and want to make an impact, here are a few thoughts I'd offer.

First, target one of the top-tier firms in your industry that you want to change. By *change* I mean build a superior business model that will elevate *all* teams. And by *superior,* I mean one that improves the lives of those *providing* the service and those *receiving* the service.

How can you tell if you have a superior model? A great indicator is when your major competitors are forced to change. Perhaps they lose market share and some of their major players join your team. While some might see this level of competition as a negative, I believe it is an obligation. If you are one of the leaders of your industry, you owe it to others in your industry to keep pace with the times and improve the service offered to customers. Otherwise, your entire industry might go obsolete. This was a principle I recognized throughout my career.

For example, at J. Walter Thompson, our president, Dan Seymour, adapted the great Bill Bernbach's creative team concept and created a totally integrated creative department. Instead of starting from scratch, Seymour looked at a model he knew would work and adapted it to fit his large organization. And thanks to his creative department concept, I doubt if there is one global ad agency on the planet that doesn't use some version of this model today. This taught me an invaluable lesson.

When I arrived at the Peace Corps, I had a chance to improve the quality of our service to our host countries around the world. I wasn't just worried about having a job or building my résumé. I wanted to make a global impact. Similarly, when I joined Jenny Craig, I had loftier visions than just growing the brand. I also wanted to have a positive impact on our nation's obesity crisis. The only way this was going to happen was if we raised the tide of all boats.

During my time at Heidrick & Struggles and Spencer Stuart, it wasn't as if I was some dynamic leader who came up with a magical system to change both companies. Rather, I took note of how the entire professional services industry was changing and worked with the brightest minds to bring these same changes to an industry that had lagged behind. In doing so, this helped our industry change for the better. For the past thirty years, both Heidrick & Struggles and Spencer Stuart have remained two of the top five executive search firms in the world.

In retrospect, the changes made in these organizations live on to this day. Global ad agencies around the world use some version of the totally integrated creative department concept. The Peace Corps Pre-Slot volunteer delivery system is still alive and well. Every SHREK firm fully embraces some version of the specialization business model. And progress is being made on a healthy lifestyle business model.

If you have already achieved career success, changing your industry is not only possible. It is a tremendous opportunity.

CHAPTER 8

CHANGE YOUR STUDENTS

B y 2003, I had far exceeded my career expectations. Life was wonderful. My wife and our two children were enjoying their careers. We were financially stable. And I felt like a sixty-five-year-old child awaiting my first day of school. While I wasn't sure what to do next, there was one thing I knew for certain: *I was going to continue being a change agent.*

You might label this obsession a divine calling. While I'm not an overly religious person, I believe in God and have spent many hours communicating with him. There is much about him I don't understand, but I'm convinced he has always been by my side. For that, I am grateful. I feel like he has given me a wonderful life, and the least I can do is give back to others.

This introspective journey took me back to where it all started: my time in college. My years at San José State were the launching pad for my career and season of personal awakening. Without life-changing career development and influential role models such as Dean Benz, I don't know what I would have become.

Throughout my career, I lived with a profound sense of gratitude to those who took time to steer me in the right direction. If the opportunity ever presented itself, I knew I wanted to have a similar impact on others. Today, we live in a country where 56 percent of university graduates are the first in their family to receive a college degree.[16] If there is any structure that could use some change, it is our models of education.

ANSWERING A CALL TO ACTION

Although I didn't retire until my seventieth birthday, as soon as I turned sixty-five, I joined the College of Business Administration Advisory Board of the business school at California State University San Marcos. I always seemed to join the largest organization in any industry, and my decision to join the teaching team at CSUSM was no exception. CSUSM is one of twenty-three state universities in the California State University system—the largest educational system in the US with more than 460,000 students. Because of its massive reach, I knew there was tremendous potential to change the lives of countless individuals.

The first couple of years on the board were quiet. But then, the 2008 global financial crisis arrived, and the CSU president announced that the entire CSU system could expect substantial budget cutbacks.

---

16   Ilana Hamilton, "56% of All Undergraduates Are First-Generation College Students," Forbes Advisor, accessed August 30, 2023, https://www.forbes.com/advisor/education/first-generation-college-students-by-state/.

This call meant all twenty-three state universities were to submit revised budgets along with adjusted enrollment and tuition projections. As a response, our Cal State San Marcos president issued a "Call to Action" alert to all five colleges in our university.

Knowing my background, the dean of the business school, Dennis Gusmann, asked if I would become chairman of his twenty-person advisory board and help him deal with this crisis. We knew the uphill battle that lay ahead, and there would be added pressure to do more with less as the California budget crisis escalated. Because the college didn't have a clear strategy in place, I suggested we create our first three-year strategic plan and incorporate new budget initiatives along with metrics of accountability. Given this was primarily a *voluntary* member board, I knew this was a big ask for our members.

Channeling my inner William Wallace of *Braveheart*, I emailed a rallying cry to our board that said, "I see this as our moment of truth. Why else did we sign up for this gig if it wasn't to answer the bell when we were needed most? Our students deserve an opportunity to earn a college degree, especially when we know that most of them work to pay for it. So let's saddle up and have some fun making a real difference."

To their credit, rather than shrink from the challenge, the board stepped up and delivered. The board was comprised of the dean's staff and leaders from the community, but I quickly added a couple of faculty members and students as well as the CFO of the university. I wanted all constituencies represented because I had a master plan in mind. I was convinced that since we were the *business school*, we had an obligation to build a new business model for other colleges within the university to use.

My intention was not only to get all colleges in our university to buy in but to get all twenty-three universities in our system to join forces. As the biggest educational system in the country, who knew what the outcome might be?

THE PLAN

Taking a page out of my executive search playbook, my next step involved collecting buy-in from key players and reinforcing our plan with solid research.

To accomplish this, I conducted a full-day, off-site conference with over thirty people, and we had a series of team-building exercises where we received productive input. Coming out of these conversations, we all recognized it was going to become increasingly competitive to recruit students. The key was to find a way we could differentiate ourselves in the marketplace to remain competitive with other public and private institutions.

Based on my marketing background at J. Walter Thompson, I knew we had to package our product in a memorable way. In this case, I felt the one key word we had to emphasize was *accountability*. Why? Think about it. How many times have you heard a public educational system talk about staff reductions and generating additional funds in the same sentence? As you would expect, they're always looking to tip the financial scales in their favor.

When I thought of great examples of accountability, my mind went to Newt Gingrich's 1994 "Contract with America." The goal of this contract was to create a binding document that told the American people precisely what they could expect if they elected a Republican-controlled House of Congress. As history shows, President Clinton embraced the substance on its merit, and it proved to right the US ship for a few years.

With this template in mind, I created "The Contract with CoBA." To kick off the program, I invited the university president, provost, CFO, department heads, and media to join my board meeting for the signing of our contracts. This step helped assure students we were serious about keeping our promises.

I can't tell you how amazing the board was through this entire process. They were willing to devote countless hours to worthwhile endeavors such as helping our public institution become more self-sufficient and use less state tax dollars to prosper. Many of our projects continue to benefit the university. An example is the "CSUSM Taste for Student Success," which is an annual fundraiser that supports student success initiatives across the school. Local wineries, breweries, and restaurants attend and serve sample tastes from their businesses. Guests enjoy tasting, live music, a silent auction, and a photo booth. In fact, the first bottle of wine ever auctioned off was a bottle of wine I made from my vineyard and winery for $285 (more on this in the next chapter).

As we were implementing what we were creating, the state magically found enough money to keep us fully funded. As a result, we did not suffer any reductions. Once that occurred, becoming more self-sufficient lost its significance. Nevertheless, enough of what we had worked on was put to good use so that we all felt our time was well spent.

Part of me was disappointed the 2008 financial crisis didn't last long enough to force us and other educational entities to create entirely new business models. As it stands, there remains a desperate need to address the growing financial challenges within our educational institutions. But as a result of our success, I was asked to join the CSUSM Foundation Board. This group consists of community leaders who support CSUSM strategic plans for growth through fundraising.

During my nine years on this board, we designed and implemented a capital campaign that raised $55 million for the university. This was an amazing success for a small public college only thirty years old.

THE JOY OF TEACHING STUDENTS

I must confess that teaching had always been in the back of my mind, and I knew it was only a matter of time before I stood in front of a classroom. Like most people, I had a couple of teachers I admired and wanted to be like. And if I had a nickel for everyone who said I should teach at some point in my life, I could have retired sooner.

The other reason I thought it was important to spend time with students was because I wanted to hear directly from them. After all, they were the ones we were serving on the Advisory Board. As my life's work has demonstrated, I always believed it was essential to know what those I was serving want to be served.

I'm thankful to David Bennett, a good friend, who recruited me to CSUSM and encouraged me to become a professor. He was teaching the career development class at CoBA, which he helped create, and felt the need to start up another class. He and I had similar corporate backgrounds and thought I would be a great fit. I thanked him by conducting the wedding ceremony for he and his wife, Geri, in my vineyard.

Initially, when Dean Dennis Gusman asked me to teach, I told him I would do it on the condition I did not receive any pay. If I was doing this to give back, I didn't want anything in return. In my mind, if I succeeded that would be payment enough. The dean smiled and said, "Not a problem." However, weeks later he informed me this arrangement was unacceptable to the teachers' union. So I decided I would find other ways to give back.

One way I knew I could do this was through creating more student engagement in career development by improving the quality of the class. To help accomplish this objective, I created a $500 career development scholarship that honored the most outstanding leadership student in my class. This award was based on the individual who recommended the best ideas that made the class better. The winner was chosen by the students, and the award was handed out by the new dean of the business school, Jim Hamerly. It worked beautifully. The suggestions were brilliant, and I still use them today. My wife and I also established an annual scholarship in our family name that's awarded to the outstanding graduate from the College of Business Administration every year.

To better understand who my students are, let me give you a few rough statistics. Over 50 percent of my students are the first in their family to attend college. Our school is ranked number one in the US in social mobility. Seventy-five percent of students work at least twenty hours a week, one-third have full-time jobs, and many have more than one job. Fifteen percent know what they want to do and how to secure the job that they want. Thirty-five percent have an idea of what they want to do but don't know how to get the right job. And 50 percent don't have a clue as to what they want to do.

My personal belief is that a third of my students listen to my advice and hear what I have to say. Another third hear me and hopefully will listen to me *later* in their career. And the last third are in need of improving their listening skills.

In my opinion, a few in this final group should consider a trade or vocational school. This path is a faster and more affordable route to a well-paying career. Not everyone belongs in a four-year educational institution. And it's not enough to merely earn a degree so you can be the first in your family to do so. There are plenty of well-paying, satis-fying career opportunities for those without four-year college degrees.

When I started, my class was optional for students. But to me, this was unacceptable. Since 95 percent of my students made it clear the number one reason they were in college was to get a good job, and because this course was designed to get them that job, I believed this course should be mandatory for all business students. As such, I knew I had to convince the rest of the faculty and administration that adding this class was justified.

My strongest asset was my students. I knew that once they were convinced every student should take this class, they would become my ambassadors. To help differentiate our class and make it special, I created a certificate for every student that passed. At the end of each semester, I conducted a fun ceremony where the dean of the business school, Jim Hamerly, was invited. Together we awarded individually framed certificates and had each student hold up their certificate and have their picture taken with the dean and me on either side.

The second part of this class was used as a forum to allow Dean Hamerly an opportunity to conduct a Q&A with my class. He would start by giving a short college status report and then ask questions about the class. *What could be changed to make it better? Should everyone in the business school be required to take it? What should be changed to make the college better?*

It took a while for others to accept my vision. Not Dean Hamerly. Thanks to his leadership and commitment, we succeeded in morphing my class into a new and improved *mandatory* class called Business Professional Development. Now over four hundred students instead of only forty receive this curriculum every semester. To celebrate, Dean Hamerly and I enjoyed competing in the 2018 USA Age-Group National Triathlon Championships.

While I never succeeded in finding a way to have this model accepted by the entire CSU system, this class continues to get better every year. It is now considered the crown jewel of the business school. At this point, I've taught and coached over a thousand students and have no plan to stop. I say "coached" because our model has two coaches assigned to every instructor. Each coach has twenty students assigned to them for mentoring purposes throughout the entire semester.

As a coach, not only do I attend and participate in classes, but I also have two hour-long individual coaching sessions with each student to go over all parts of the course and their career action plan. When COVID-19 hit, I began coaching because I hated teaching online. Without the human interaction and lively discussion generated from healthy Q&A exchanges, I found the lack of engagement disappointing. So I moved over to coaching but plan to return to teaching next semester.

I love the relationships I've built with so many students. Some I've mentored for years with the longest of these being Maggie Pilgram. We've met regularly for over thirteen years. Maggie is now on the CoBA Advisory Board where I first started with the college and has had a terrific career with one of the leading recruiting organizations in the world.

The most fulfilling part of teaching is receiving a note or holiday card from a former student bringing me up to date on their career and sharing how much I impacted their success. I was fortunate to receive many of these communications in my professional life, but there's something special when you receive it from someone you helped get started.

In fifteen years, I've never turned away a student from entering my class. I started teaching three weeks after I retired at seventy and am still doing it at eighty-five. I can't wait to look on the faces of my new students next semester when I introduce myself on our first day and say, "I sat in your chair just *sixty* years ago." While many things change with age, there are timeless principles that remain the same.

MY TEN CAREER COMMANDMENTS

To this point, one of the most common questions students and those in business ask is, "What are the guiding principles that should shape my career?"

While I can't say I've ever been to the top of Mount Sinai and received a list of instructions on tablets of stone, I can say there are ten principles, or commandments, that have shaped my life. And it's these same commandments I share with students. They are as follows:

COMMANDMENT #1: KNOW YOURSELF AND BE YOURSELF

- Know who you are.

- Stay true to yourself.

- Do what's best for you.

It was Aristotle who said, "Knowing yourself is the beginning of all wisdom." Maybe your story is like mine and you spent a lot of time by yourself as a kid. But if you're like most American young adults today, you've spent large portions of your childhood on social media and consuming digital entertainment. As such you might struggle to sit alone in silence and be comfortable in your own skin. If this is your story, your challenge will be to grow comfortable with who you are when no one else is watching, and then be that person at all times and in all places. The better you know yourself, the better chance you have of fulfilling your dreams.

COMMANDMENT #2: REALIZE YOUR DESTINY IS UP TO YOU

- Take control by creating a plan.

- Develop a brand for competitive advantage.

- Never underestimate your potential.

There is an old saying: "The harder you work, the luckier you get." Yes, timing is important. But don't sit back and wait for that perfect opportunity. Instead, act and create your own breaks. It's up to you how far you go.

COMMANDMENT #3: FOCUS ON WHAT YOU LOVE MOST AND DO BEST

- Let passion be your guide.

- Blend avocation and vocation whenever possible.

- Pursue work-life integration.

You can only do a few things with excellence. No two of us are alike. We all have special gifts that differ from others. So find yours and blend it with your avocation and vocation. For me, I am a change agent. I can see what needs to be done, listen to the right people, and craft a plan that will take us from A to B. This is what I do, and this is what I love. But what about you? What are you most passionate about? How can you blend your avocation and vocation? If so, you'll never work another day in your life.

COMMANDMENT #4: EXCEED EXPECTATIONS AND GO THE EXTRA MILE

- Always try to do your best.

- Build professional character with strong work ethics.

- Remember that you can have it all by earning it.

I was never the smartest guy in my class. But in many respects, I think this worked to my advantage. Instead of being a student of words, I became a student of people. Because I wasn't the 4.0 GPA graduate from Harvard, I realized I needed to work twice as hard to compete with others who had more natural ability. The same is true for you. Talent only takes you so far. You must have a strong work ethic to back it up. Few things in life pay greater dividends.

COMMANDMENT #5: BUILD YOUR NETWORK BY CULTIVATING RELATIONSHIPS

- Who you know can impact how high you go.

- Most jobs come from professional networking.

- Use your mentors as your career advisory board.

It's worth reiterating that I didn't receive *one* job without relationships. From J. Walter Thompson to the Peace Corps to Heidrick & Struggles to Spencer Stuart to Jenny Craig and even to teaching at California State University San Marcos, each opportunity came about because of critical relationships I'd formed. The same will likely be true for you. While you might think of yourself as someone who isn't a people person, let me encourage you to adjust your mindset. It's OK to be an introvert like me. But if you want to succeed in your career, you must learn how to build relationships. Yes, this might feel unnatural, but you can do it. It's a life-long process that must be learned.

COMMANDMENT #6: ACHIEVE GOALS BY MANAGING TIME EFFECTIVELY

- Maintain a daily "to do" list.

- Never lose sight of your priorities.

- Become a lean, mean, efficient machine.

We've all got the same number of hours in a day. But what separates highly successful people from others is time management. As author James Clear notes, "You do not rise to the level of your goals. You fall to the level of your systems."[17] Having goals is great. But having effective daily systems is even better. A basic system to implement is taking five minutes each evening to plan tomorrow's agenda. Make the time to reach your potential.

COMMANDMENT #7: SPECIALIZE TO STRENGTHEN YOUR BRAND

- You need to become very good at something.

- Specialization rules the professional services world.

- Generalists still have a path, but it's narrowing.

It would be hard for me to have a Top Ten Career Commandments list without talking about specialization. Yes, there will always be a need for generalists, but as our world grows closer together and consumers have more options, the need for specialization will only increase. It's easy to become an expert in something you love.

---

17   James Clear, "You Do Not Rise to the Level of Your Goals. You Fall to the Level of Your Systems," accessed August 23, 2023, https://jamesclear.com/quotes/you-do-not-rise-to-the-level-of-your-goals-you-fall-to-the-level-of-your-systems.

COMMANDMENT #8: CHANGE THINGS FOR THE BETTER

- Every organization and every person can be better.

- You can work harder, smarter, or closer together.

- Walk the walk by showing you care.

In every work environment you face, you should ask yourself one question: *How can I change my organization for the better?* Regardless of your place on the organizational chart, there is always *something* you can do. And as you do, remember my advice to work closer together.

COMMANDMENT #9: BE A ROLE MODEL FOR OTHERS

- Your life partner can make a big difference.

- Be what you want others to become.

- Role models can serve as effective change agents.

You should live a life that inspires others to be better. This doesn't mean you have a long list of grand accomplishments. But there should be something about you that motivates others to be better. This includes your own family.

COMMANDMENT #10: KEEP GROWING BY ALWAYS LEARNING

- What doesn't grow will die.

- Staying competitive requires continual learning.

- Develop your own career commandments.

That which does not grow will die. This means that if you want to remain at the top of your game, you will need to be a continuous learner. The pace at which most industries change today is breathtaking. And refusing to adapt with the times can render yourself and your organization obsolete.

This is my list. It's what has worked for me. But I'd encourage you to make your own. Write down your non-negotiables that will shape your interactions with others. Then follow through by living your life in sync with these core values.

MY FAVORITE STUDENTS

Ultimately, what made my class so successful was not me, not the dean, and not the college. It was the students. It was their voices that needed to be heard. They created the demand, and I merely helped ignite, channel, and showcase their desires.

My message to students has always been that their careers were indeed *theirs* for the taking. While listening to guys like me might be helpful, it was up to them to take control of their destiny. In thirty years when they look at themselves in the mirror, I want them to shoulder the credit or blame for what they have or have not achieved.

As the creator of the original class, Troy Nielson, often said, "Your degree is an important step but is only an admission ticket to the dance. You still need to pick the right dance partner, keep learning new dance steps and package yourself in such a way that somebody will want to dance with you."[18]

If you were to ask me if I have a favorite student, I would say I'm partial to veterans. Currently, our college is home to over 400 student veterans—the highest percentage per capita of any California state campus. We also serve close to two thousand military-connected students, which is 12 percent of our campus population. In each of

---

18   Troy R. Nielson, *Career Trek* (Hoboken, NJ: Prentice Hall, 2007).

the thirty-plus classes I've taught and coached, close to 10 percent of my students were veterans.

From day one, I found veteran students among the most attentive. One of the reasons is because they naturally realized how serious this course was for their life. Many had been through combat, struggled with post-traumatic stress, and had a difficult time finding work.

Starting with my first class, my veteran students encouraged me to teach my class in the Veterans Center on campus or to teach it at Camp Pendleton for veterans leaving the military. Nearly every one of them had buddies who couldn't find meaningful work and now struggled with homelessness and suicide. What they needed was a blueprint for how to move forward.

The more they talked, the more I felt guilty for not doing something. Still, I held back. Then, one day, everything changed.

CHAPTER 9

CHANGE YOUR VETERANS

O ne morning after the end of my lecture, a veteran approached and apologized for not making my last class the previous week. As it turned out, he had a traumatic reason for his absence. He had woken up that morning to discover his roommate, who was also a veteran, had hanged himself in their bathroom.

Listening to my student share, I felt sick to my stomach and my mind recalled all the times I'd had an opportunity to help veterans in my school but clearly hadn't done enough. That moment, I vowed things would be different. The next day I met with the dean and asked how we could arrange for me to teach my class to all veterans on campus.

I offered to teach my class in the CoBA conference room where I could reach 120 veterans at a time. And bless his soul, Dean Hamerly did everything he could. But that's when politics raised its ugly head again and my idea was blocked.

Thinking back to my student who had lost his roommate, I thought to myself, *To hell with getting blocked from doing the right thing*, and I took matters into my own hands. I decided to create a 501(c)(3) tax exempt organization and create a business model that would match veterans with the career jobs they wanted, where they wanted, and with the support needed to make them successful. Sound ambitious? You're darned right. But I was going to do my best.

After all, why not? Big problems require big solutions, and no one on this planet is more deserving than our veterans.

THE REASONS I LOVE VETERANS

I have always admired our veterans. Even though I was never activated to serve in battle, I was proud of my service as an Army National Guardsman. As I shared in chapter 3, I remember being packed and on twenty-four-hour alert during basic training when the Cuban Missile Crisis erupted. While President Kennedy avoided a war, that love and sense of camaraderie for my fellow brothers and sisters in the military never left. I knew that if I ever had the chance, I was going to find a way to continue my service and give back to those who had given so much.

My wife had four uncles, and each of them served, as did my aunt and uncle. My uncle was a marine sergeant who was badly wounded at Iwo Jima, and my aunt Snookie served as a WAVE (Women Accepted for Volunteer Emergency Service). She was something special. While training in New York, she won a jitterbug contest in the Empire State

Building and the base training typing contest by typing 115 words a minute on a manual typewriter without any errors. One of my first memories at five years of age was seeing her in uniform when she was on leave. The military was an embedded part of my upbringing. Even my first vehicle was a green WWII jeep that my uncle purchased for me when I was in high school.

There is something special about veterans. As a teacher, I always found the veterans in my class among the most engaged. After serving one or two tours of duty, they have a true sense of purpose when they enter college. The biggest problem I have with them is when I can't get them to call me "Ron" instead of "Sir." There is no greater feeling than helping veterans transition into the business world.

One of the things I've always loved about veterans is that I can always count on them as a go-to source for honest feedback. As a new teacher, I wanted to get everyone on board and see no student left behind. It always pains me if I feel students aren't giving it their all. For example, last semester, I had a coaching session scheduled for an early morning Zoom call with a student. It had been scheduled for over a month, and he had plenty of reminders. But when our time arrived, he wasn't on screen. Knowing his phone never left his side, I gave him several calls. Finally, on the third try, I received a sleepy, "Hello?"

"John," I said, "you have five minutes." To his credit, he refocused, and we had a wonderful session.

When I first started teaching, my goal was always 100 percent engagement, and I grew frustrated with students who didn't put in the effort. One morning, I was especially agitated with lack of student engagement and began venting my frustrations to the class. But that's when one of the veterans raised his hand and said, "Sir, there will always be a certain percentage of your students who just don't give a sh*t!"

His point hit home. And after thanking him, I moved on with my lesson.

While some look at the unique struggles veterans face and throw up their hands, I see this as a challenge. Whenever possible, I try to set veterans up for success. As a teacher, whenever I have my class form teams, I try to match students of similar backgrounds or interests. One time, I matched two ex-cons. One was a female veteran who had gotten into some trouble after transitioning out of the military, and the other was a young man who had held up a pharmacy with a BB gun. Both had served time and were trying to get back on their feet.

I knew their stories because each had approached me early in the semester and asked for personal counseling. Both were having difficulty finding a job because of their criminal records, and they wanted advice. Knowing these were good people who had just made a few wrong decisions, I asked them to quietly work together outside of class. Over the next several months, I watched their friendship form as they privately assisted others who were struggling. Both found jobs soon after graduation.

Sometimes it's the individuals who carry the most baggage who are best positioned to go the furthest in life. They've built their mental fortitude but just need someone to steer them in the right direction.

GETTING THE BALL ROLLING

After trying everything in my power to transport my class to the Veterans Center but still coming up short, I shifted my approach. Rather than trying to reach only the 350–450 veterans on campus, I decided to broaden my target to the entire 150,000 veterans transitioning out of the US military every year.

To get the ball rolling, I teamed up with my good friend Bill Hixson, who has since passed away. Bill was instrumental in designing the Peace Corps Pre-Slot model and may have been the most intelligent person I ever knew. I have always surrounded myself with people smarter than me (my wife being the primary example), and this guy was no exception. A 1,600 on his college SAT, Rensselaer Polytechnic Institute BS, Harvard MBA, Columbia PhD, and two master's degrees certainly qualified him for my team.

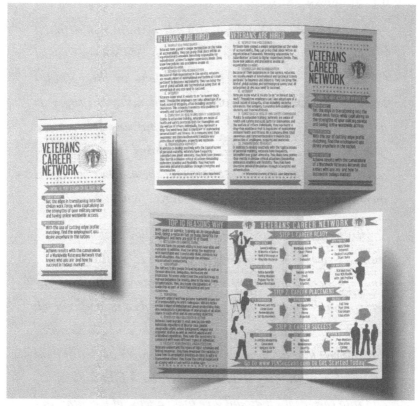

Mock-up brochure for the Veterans Career Network (VCN) organization, 2012

It is true that one of the smartest things a leader can do is surround himself with people that are smarter than he is.

Together, we began the laborious process of applying for a nonprofit 501(c)(3) organization IRS approval. We also began to design the business model for our organization, which we planned to call "Veterans Career Network" (VCN). My goal was to incorporate the best pieces of the ideas and models I had accumulated over the years and tailor them to work for veterans in the present day. These were proven practices that still work today, and I was certain they would work with helping veterans find employment. The summary of our plan looked like this:

> *Historically, veterans have struggled during transition to find a meaningful job on a potential career path. My proposed model (VCN) is designed to find 120,000+ jobs for the 150,000 veterans who are transitioning out of the military every year without one. (30,000 don't need or want any help.) More specifically, my model will help transitioning veterans find the career jobs they want, where they want them, when they need them most, and with the support resources to be successful.*
>
> *Studies for decades have pointed to unemployment and homelessness as two of the top reasons for veterans committing suicide. And my model will help solve both problems as well as our veterans' underemployment nightmare. We do a magnificent job of transitioning civilians into military jobs and have created the strongest fighting force on the planet. But we obviously need help with transitioning service members back into civilian life and into career jobs that will give them a sense of meaning and purpose. Accomplishing this is not the complete answer, but we will never make any significant progress until this phase is available and properly used.*

I realized this was a tall order and I was going to need some help.

COLLECTING INPUT

To build an effective model, it was imperative to meet with those for whom the model was being built. Owning a vineyard and winery (more on this in the next chapter), I conducted most of my research over glasses of wine with members of every branch in the military. This included generals and privates, young and old, men and women. I also paid close attention to those working in the Veterans Administration.

For younger veterans, the story was often the same. I once asked ten of them seated at my table, "Why did you join the military?"

Their collective response? "9/11." The terrorist attacks of that day proved just the motivation to make them sign up and defend their country. Most had signed on for multiple tours and had a level of patriotism and commitment to service I find in short supply today.

I met with multiple veteran service organizations to see what they were doing regarding career development and job placement. As I discovered, there were thousands of them throughout our county that were doing wonderful things for our veterans. However, there was a problem. For reasons unknown to me, most refused to share resources and intellectual capital with each other. And almost all were locally or regionally focused.

For months, I did whatever I could to get in front of as many veterans as possible. I even purchased the top $4,000 CSUSM auction gift at our annual college fundraising dinner to get a personalized tour of Camp Pendleton and introductions to some of the officers I wanted as part of my Veterans Career Network team. Our tour guide was Major General Tony Jackson, one of the former commanding generals of the marine base and someone I was recruiting to be on my board. In fact, his former chief of staff was already on. The tour included my wife and other members of my board and was one of the most exciting and rewarding days of our lives.

Experiences like these gave me the invaluable feedback I needed to see my plan come to life. There were so many benefits to successfully transitioning veterans back into civilian life and helping them get on the right career path. The obvious one was the help it would provide for veterans. But a second benefit was military recruitment.

In an era with record recruitment lows, it's a tough sell to ask young adults to dedicate some of their prime years to serving a nation that doesn't help them get back on their feet. However, if veterans knew they could count on a smooth transition back into civilian life with a career job after serving our country, I believe we would experience a significant increase in our voluntary enrollment.

I believed this in 2011, and I believe it more than ever today.

A ROADBLOCK

At first, everything was headed in the right direction. I had a clear plan, the right team players, and the proper connections to make an impact. But then, an unexpected roadblock.

After submitting my 501(c)(3) to the IRS in 2012, I was told it should only take about four months to get approved. There was no reason to think it wouldn't be. The plan was comprehensive, I had a proven track record, and we had a long list of notable military figures who supported our concept. But after several months, I heard nothing, and it soon became clear we would not be approved. Unbeknownst to me, politics had reared its ugly head once again.

As was later discovered, certain members within the IRS were responsible for targeting conservative groups and rejecting their nonprofit applications. If you'll recall, the IRS official in charge of the division that targeted conservative groups was Lois Lerner, and on May 22, 2013, she was asked to testify in front of Congress. In her opening statement, Lerner said she had not broken any laws or IRS rules and that she would plead the Fifth Amendment for all questions she received.[19]

Sitting on my couch in Rancho Santa Fe, I watched these hearings with great interest. As I did, everything became clear. Even though I was almost entirely apolitical, my name was still attached to the Nixon and Ford administrations. Despite the fact that my nonprofit had nothing to do with politics, I realized my submission was blocked because of ulterior political motivations.

On September 23, 2013, Lois Lerner resigned from the IRS and eventually acknowledged an "error in judgment."[20] On April 18, 2014, my application was finally approved. But by then, it was too late for my nonprofit. It had been almost two years since I'd submitted my initial application. By now, my board was dissolved, the staff dispersed, and all the momentum we'd created was lost. All because of politics.

THE THREE PHASES OF THE VETERANS CAREER NETWORK

The rest of this chapter is devoted to any of you who might have the time and energy to advance this ball forward at a regional or local level. You can build on what I've started. And it's my hope that through sharing some of the details of my Veterans Career Network that you're inspired to action.

I've already established why a new model for veterans is necessary, but I thought it would be helpful to go into a little more detail and explain the ins and outs of *how* this model could operate. My model

---

19   YouTube, "IRS Official Lois Lerner Invokes Fifth Amendment," CBS News, May 22, 2013, https://www.youtube.com/watch?v=Z4qjZHiB54s&ab_channel=CBSNews.

20   *USA Today*, "IRS Apologizes for Targeting Conservative Groups during 2012 Election," accessed September 6, 2023, https://www.usatoday.com/story/news/politics/2013/05/10/irs-apology-conservative-groups-2012-election/2149939/.

is based on four key networks—the military, education, business, and veterans. Each network plays an essential role and is dependent on the others to achieve its mission.

VETERANS CAREER NETWORK

STEP 1. CAREER READY

What Now?	vcnsuccess.com	VCN Profile
Served in Military: 36 Months of Service, Medical Discharge, or Honorable Discharge	Worldwide Access Via: Smart Phone Tablet Computer	MOS/Skills Interest Desired Location Start Date

Transition Modules	VCN Contact	Job Matches
Online Gamified Training Modules Prepare You for Civilian Workforce	Receive an Intro Email, Phone Call, & Letter	VCN Matches Your VCN Profile with Job Profiles All Online.

STEP 2. CAREER PLACEMENT

VCN Orientation	Interview/s	Receive Job
Network with Vets Career Coach Review Matches Set Up Interview/s	Vet Supportive: Video Phone In-person	Full Time Part Time Paid Intern Education

STEP 3. CAREER SUCCESS

Sustainability	VCN Events	Veteran Network
Lifetime Membership Camaraderie Navigate the VA Give Back!	Network Development Benefits Life Skills	Peer Mentors Education Career VA Benefits

Mock-up brochure for the Veterans Career Network organization, 2012

This model has three phases.

In phase I, the military will help prepare service members for transition. At the close of their time in the service, veterans will need to decide whether they are positioned to take an immediate job or if they need more education to meet the base qualifications. VCN will then help them make that decision. If there are no adequate job matches available, the veteran should return to school. That said, active-duty service members and veterans need to be reminded this is only a *temporary* phase and that unemployment should not be an option. Nevertheless, this is their best decision for now.

In phase II, education and business will work together to help veterans get the right job. Through working with local chambers of commerce, veterans will be paired with potential employers who are willing to hire them. If further education is required by the hiring entity, VCN will work with them to agree on what additional education is needed and find a student veteran attending the same educational institution to serve as a mentor.

In phase III, veterans will help other veterans succeed in their jobs. Once a veteran is hired, VCN will identify other veterans to be their support coaches or mentors. This is like the kind of support needed when a veteran transitions into an educational institution.

The chambers of commerce play a pivotal role in this model. Each chamber will work with its member companies to identify existing and future jobs that they would be interested in filling with qualified veterans. From there, companies would post their job specs online asking interested veterans to submit their résumés for consideration. Companies would then initiate communication with those applicants they wish to pursue.

The next step is sufficient referencing and screening. From there, companies would decide to:

- Hire the veteran,

- Not hire the veteran, or

- Ask the veteran to supplement his or her qualifications with additional schooling.

If additional schooling is required, this can be achieved while the veteran starts work or interns with the company. Another option is for the veteran to return to school full time and reapply at an appropriate future date. If the veteran returns to school, it would be the responsibility of that school to pair the veteran up with another veteran who can act as a mentor within that educational environment.

The college or university would also make sure the veteran receives the specific academic curriculum agreed to by the hiring company or chamber. Once in their new job, the model would see to it that another veteran in a similar job elsewhere in the country becomes a career mentor. This matching would be done online with videos and additional training support being part of the mentoring process.

THE ROLES OF VETERANS AND COMPANIES

A unique and powerful part of the VCN process is the role veterans play in each phase. To start, the goal was for all VCN members to be veterans. They would design the entire process. Veterans would help recruit and process all candidates, and veterans would help mentor during the screening, educating, and on-the-job counseling phases. In my mind, the dedication and commitment of one veteran helping another veteran succeed has no equal.

I knew veterans would want to be involved, but what about businesses? Why would companies partner with VCN to help fill open jobs with veterans? Here were a few reasons I thought they would:

- First, VCN would help them hire veterans they want with the skills they need.

- Second, VCN would help them identify, recruit, process, develop, place, and mentor each veteran.

- Third, VCN would assure their veterans are vetted and mentored by other veterans.

- Fourth, VCN would assist companies in offsetting all expenses with federal tax credits. For all of this, VCN could charge up to $4,000 per veteran hired (which is the national minimum average hiring cost per employee).

There are many ways hiring entities can take advantage of the tax credits associated with hiring veterans to reduce the actual cost. In any case, I truly believed our employer-based approach to creating career opportunities for veterans who completed this process would exceed the expectations of our corporate partners.

For decades, many companies have been willing to hire veterans, and veterans have been eager to be hired. But neither have had a viable process to achieve their mission. Millions of dollars and hours have been spent on this ever-increasing problem. *Most have approached the problem by focusing on how to find the right job for a veteran, rather than finding the right veteran for a job.*

This might seem like a subtle difference, but it is *the* difference. When you are trying to match someone's interests, skills, and experience for a job, but they have little or no direct experience in that role, you must rely on a vetting process that helps each party fully understand the qualifications and expectations of the other.

During my time with the Peace Corps, everything changed when I shifted to finding the right people for the right roles. This changed the entire mindset of everyone involved and brought clarity to the entire process. Every metric used to evaluate the quality of the program improved beyond anyone's expectations.

PLAN OF IMPLEMENTATION

While this plan I've outlined could work in any region of the United States, my goal was to start locally by building a prototype in San Diego. Here is what I envisioned this could look like.

Step 1 | Recruit four to eight San Diego companies with available job openings to participate.

Step 2 | Work with different companies' job descriptions to translate individual characteristics into a common set of characteristics to provide profiles that veterans can fill.

Step 3 | Identify forty to fifty service members at Camp Pendleton who have these common characteristics and would be willing to participate in this prototype.

Step 4 | Once the service member and company decide there is enough of a match to explore the opportunity further, an initial screening or interview would be conducted via phone or Zoom.

Step 5 | If the service member and company further agree that a tentative match exists, VCN would arrange for both to meet to conduct formal interviewing and to address any qualification gaps that might exist. Employment options would be discussed, along with additional education requirements, if needed.

Step 6 | If additional education and skills development were necessary, VCN would recommend a specific package of educational courses and counseling to fill in the gap of required job qualifications.

Step 7 | Once an employment agreement is reached, VCN would identify and recruit a peer veteran to work with the VCN veteran at the school or the company. Ideally, the peer education veteran would be at the same school. Likewise, the peer career veteran would be successfully performing in a similar job in the same industry and in the same geographic area.

Step 8 | VCN would periodically contact the company and the veteran to monitor job performance and career progress.

In the appendix, I've included three charts that include the following: (A) a matrix of the entire military to civilian career transition model, (B) a flow chart of the veteran process, and (C) the first page of the service member process to show the exact steps each veteran would take. A similarly detailed process would be created for the other three networks: business, education, and military.

Since Camp Pendleton is close by and marines are one of the most difficult branches to transition back into civilian life, I chose them to build my prototype around. I was fortunate enough to recruit Lt. Colonel Mike Naylor (former chief of staff of a camp commander) and General Mel Spiese, who oversaw all training on the base. Both were ready to play an integral part of my program. Another reason for choosing Camp Pendleton was because many of my students were stationed there while taking my class.

In addition, I spoke with the US Chamber of Commerce as well as several local chapters who were very supportive of my concept. I also spoke with the creators of Match.com, one of the largest and most sophisticated matching-people platforms in the world. The president graciously said that they would consider doing their part by helping me build our technology platform and website.

And lastly, I intended to explore a potential partnership with, in my opinion, the most successful veterans transition company in the San Diego market who possesses an O*NET-based transferable skills system that considers a person's functional capacities, interests, and current labor market information when conducting career research.

SUMMARY OF WHY VCN IS DIFFERENT

In summary, there are several reasons I believe a program like VCN could be very effective.

- First, we wouldn't find jobs for veterans. We would find veterans for jobs. A big difference.

- Second, our process would match veterans with a career job they want, where they want it, when they need it most, along with the support needed to succeed.

- Third, our process would include every component necessary for success: military, veterans, companies, schools, and mentors.

- Fourth, we would work with companies to identify specific career job opportunities for which they would be willing to hire veterans.

- Fifth, we would engage veterans who are interested in exploring these opportunities.

- Sixth, we would create potential matches and facilitate a process whereby both parties explore potential, interest, and possible gaps in qualifications, realizing there is seldom a perfect match.

- Seventh, if additional schooling or skills development were necessary, we would coordinate the creation of a supplement education package that, if agreed to by the veteran and company, becomes an employment agreement by both parties.

- Eighth, we would provide a formalized mentoring program whereby we matched peer veterans with our VCN veteran at their school and job.

Some days I look back to 2011 and think about what could have been if politics hadn't gotten in the way. How many more veterans would be employed today? What could this mean for their personal self-esteem and the livelihood of their families? And how might this have changed the tide of recruitment?

But as someone who likes to think toward the future, it's here I turn to you, the reader, and issue a challenge. Maybe you're a veteran or someone who is passionate about helping veterans. Regardless, you're in a position where you want to make a difference. But maybe you've just needed the right inspiration to get started. If so, I hope this chapter motivates you to action. I challenge you to take this concept and run with it. See where it might take you and the good you can accomplish.

While I know this chapter is a bit of a twist from the other nine, I didn't see how I could write this book without it. I'm proud of what I've changed in the past, but if there is one final change I could influence in some way, this would be it. Obviously, I can't possibly know who all will read this book, but my hope is that maybe, just maybe, this chapter becomes the impetus for something great.

CHAPTER 10

CHANGE YOUR RETIREMENT

Now that I'm eighty-five, I think I'm more than qualified to write about changing your retirement. While most can't wait to retire so they can stop working, I couldn't wait to retire so I could challenge myself at a higher level.

I continued to want to help others, such as my work with veterans and students, as well as corporate leaders. But I also wanted to focus on some new personal objectives. As it turned out, turning off the earning jets and focusing more on the joy of giving back was exhilarating. I felt as if my tank was refueled, and I was ready to test how high I could fly.

While there are many books written on how to make the most of one's career, few offer a clear game plan for retiring well. For some, retirement means their best years are behind them. But for me, retirement was a time to test my limitations. As I thought about how I wanted to spend my remaining years, I knew I wanted to spend them testing the boundaries of my physical, intellectual, and spiritual capacities.

CHANGING MY PHYSICAL LIMITATIONS

This testing of my physical limitations started when I was in my late thirties. I had always been an athlete and was one of the 17 million Americans that picked up *The Complete Book of Running* by James Fixx. After reading a few chapters, I started running. I was thirty-eight at the time, and by sixty-five I'd run seven marathons and dozens of other races.

Despite being young, I struggled and can remember the first time I went out for a mile-long run. My thirty-eight-year-old body felt like it was seventy-eight. Come to think of it, I ran a faster mile when I was seventy-eight than when I was age thirty-eight! I have never been a fast runner. My son could run six-minute miles with ease while I struggled getting to average eight-minute miles in marathons. Still, my most positive trait as a runner was persistence, and I could endure pain while others quit.

In 1980, I signed up for the Culver City Marathon. I entered this race only intending to run a half marathon. I'd never run more than eight miles at one time in my life and knew it wasn't wise to run a longer race than I had run in practice. Nevertheless, I couldn't wait any longer and was set on completing the 13.1 miles required.

The entire marathon had four 6.5-mile loops, and by sheer guts and determination, I finished the second loop and hit my goal.

But then something happened. The professional runners who were twice as fast as me were completing the *full* marathon just as I hit the halfway point. As I crossed the line, the roar of the crowd energized me to keep going as far as I possibly could. The next thing I knew, I had done three loops. However, I was in so much pain that I foolishly thought I might never want to endure this ever again. So I decided to go for the full marathon.

At twenty-one miles my heart started doing funny things, and as bad as I wanted to finish, I knew this race wasn't worth dying over. Calling it quits, I hobbled over the curb to sit down. Suddenly, a small elderly lady stopped running, walked over to me, and said, "Come on, sonny, you've come this far. You can't quit now! Let's run together." And we did.

After crossing the finishing line, I laid down on the lawn, completely covered in white salt, dehydrated beyond belief and unable to get to the water station only a few feet away. Thankfully, someone saw the condition I was in and brought me a drink. Slowly, my heart rate returned to normal, and I hobbled over to the tent where they were holding the awards ceremony. The last award handed out that day was to the oldest participant who finished the race. It was the lady who had rescued me. She was eighty-four.

That moment was a reality check, and I vowed to myself that I'd be in much better shape for the next marathon. The next two days, I could barely walk and slept for eighteen hours, much to Rosalie's chagrin. But that first marathon motivated me to do more, and over the next twenty-five years, I'd run six more marathons and dozens of shorter races. The Boston Marathon was the most historic and prestigious, New York was the biggest and most fun, and Los Angeles was the closest to home. I ran most with my kids, which made the experience one to remember for our entire family.

FACING THE TRIATHLON CHALLENGE

As soon as I turned sixty-five, I knew I wanted to push my physical limitations and tackle an even greater challenge—a triathlon. Triathlons are a completely different category, especially when you start training for them in your sixties. But in my mind, this was the ultimate challenge.

When I first started working toward this goal, all I knew how to do was dog-paddle across a swimming pool, and I hadn't been on a bike in half a century. Since an Ironman required a 2.4-mile swim, a 112-mile bike ride, and a 26.2-mile marathon, it seemed like the perfect challenge to test my physical limitations.

Knowing I needed some outside help, I hired a personal trainer. The running part wasn't difficult because of my experience with marathons. However, I now had to learn how to run a marathon *after* ten hours of swimming and biking.

Swimming was brutal. At my first lesson, my coach asked me to swim in the pool for as long as I could. Following her instructions, I jumped in and splashed around the pool for a whole five minutes. As I flailed about, I thought my lungs were on fire, which was strange because I swallowed nearly half the pool.

My coach smiled and said, "Great start. Our challenge is to get that five minutes up to two hours." Not double or triple the time, but *twenty-four* times more than I'd done that day. As soon as she said this, there was part of me that said this was impossible. But over the next few months, I gradually increased my time. First ten minutes, then fifteen, and then a hundred.

The biking part was hilarious, and I felt like a little kid trying to ride a tricycle. How I escaped breaking any bones I will never know. For the first year, I had a miserable time trying to get my cleated shoes free from the pedals to stand when I stopped the bike. It was so embarrassing, and I even did it once in a race when I almost fell into my wife's arms as she stood near the finish line cheering me on. Eventually, after countless scrapes and bruises, I overcame my pedal phobia.

Ironically, it was my bike that helped me win my first triathlon. When I moved into the eighty to eighty-four age group, the first race I signed up for was the San Diego Triathlon Classic. Why? Because the bike part follows the Pacific Ocean out to Point Loma and then goes straight up the sea cliff to the top. When I say straight up, I mean *straight up*. At first, you roar along the ocean at twenty-plus miles an hour in your fastest gear. Then, you make a U-turn and downshift to your lowest gear and climb the hill going two to three miles an hour. Dozens of riders are forced to get off their bike and walk it up the hill.

Older folks hate the race because of this hill, but I saw it as my chance to win my age group. Apparently, I made the right call because when the announcer handed out the awards for my category, he introduced me as the only winner who swept his age group and came in first, second, and third. My competitive strategy had worked.

Since most guys I compete against have been doing triathlons for over thirty years, I must satisfy my competitive juices in creative ways to feel I'm in the game. This underscored my overall triathlon competitive strategy from day one, which has been to outlive my competition.

My training process was an amazing experience. I'd reach a point and swear there was no way I could go any further. But then, a month later I was doing five more minutes of swimming, five more miles of biking, or five more minutes of weightlifting. This process taught me I *could* do things I thought were impossible. All I needed was patience and belief in myself that I could do more.

MY FIRST TRIATHLON

My first triathlon was like my first marathon, a near disaster. There I was in my wet suit, treading water in the middle of Mission Bay and waiting for the gun to go off. Because I wanted to get a quick start, I was in the front group. But when the gun went off, all sixty racers behind me decided that the quickest route to the finish was *over* me. And I mean that literally.

First a knee in the back, next a hand that grabbed my cap off my head, then an elbow that knocked off my goggles. To top it all off, I had two guys swim directly over me as I swallowed half of Mission Bay below.

I thought for a moment I was in serious trouble, and when I surfaced I headed straight for the shore. I was done, and this was clearly not my sport. But like the little old lady that wouldn't let me quit on my first marathon, there was an official riding a surfboard near us. His job was to watch over safety, and when he saw what had happened to me, he paddled over and asked where I was going.

"Home," I coughed, "I've had enough." But this gentleman had other ideas.

"You're here in the water," he said. "Don't give up. I know you can do it. I'll help you."

Unbeknownst to me, triathlon rules allowed swimmers to catch their breath by grabbing on to a surfboard, so long as they weren't propelled forward. For the next few hundred meters, this man stayed alongside me and became the motivational support I needed. Since that point, I've finished twenty-five of the twenty-eight triathlons I've entered, and only once have I touched a surfboard since.

Having the goal to outlive my competition, I took great pride in competing as an older participant. I'll never forget one of my first triathlons. Before you start, race organizers write your age on your calves and upper arms. As I neared the end of a thirty-two-mile Olympic distance race and could almost see the finish line ahead, I sensed someone coming alongside me. As he began to pass, he exclaimed, "Holy sh*t! You're older than my grandfather, and I'm just now passing you."

I smiled and wanted to say, "That's right, young man, and if it wasn't for my leg injury, you would have never seen me today!" But courtesy got the better of me, and I gave him a grin instead.

The more I trained, the faster I got. After a few years, I placed second in the US National Sprint competition for my age category, earning me a spot on the USA Age-Group Triathlon sprint team. Accomplishing this feat was surreal because I never dreamed I'd be competing against the world's best in anything, let alone triathlons.

My Ironman attempts didn't go well. The first ended at the hundred-mile marker when I was literally blown off my bike after eight hours of wind gusts up to seventy miles per hour. The second ended when I hit an orange street cone and flipped my bike and me into a bloody heap. At that point, I decided to forget the Ironman distance and save my body to become one of the few ninety-year-olds in history to complete an official sprint distance triathlon in competition. Besides, this was also consistent with my competitive strategy of outliving my competition.

Finish line at 2019 World Age-Group Triathlon Championships in Lausanne, Switzerland

The 2019 World Age-Group Triathlon Championships Final in Lausanne, Switzerland, was my introduction to world competition. It was a marvelous event with over five thousand triathletes from fifty nations competing in fifteen different age groups from eighteen to eighty-five. The celebration the night before the event made me feel like I was at the Olympics. There was everything from a parade to flag waving, media interviews, and fireworks, all situated on the shores of beautiful Lake Geneva. It was absolutely majestic.

Since we were in Switzerland, the race was one of the hardest I'd ever attempted. The swim was in Lake Geneva, which is melted snow. The bike ride had hills difficult to *walk*, let alone *ride*. And the route for running had handrails along the side to help walkers climb the side of the mountain.

Still, despite the challenge, the feeling of national pride was beyond description, and having most of my family there to be a part of it was amazing. Having my son-in-law give me competitive biking updates and my daughter cheer me on while running on the sidelines to the finish line was very special. While COVID-19 took me out of the last World Triathlon Sprint Championships held in Montreal, I hope to compete later this year in the eighty-five to eighty-nine age group in Malaga, Spain.

THE SCIENTIST MAKES WINE

Along with stretching myself *physically*, I wanted to stretch myself *intellectually*. According to the Myers-Briggs personality assessment, I'm classified as a "scientist." Personally, I never quite understood this because I had never made anything with my hands and never did well in chemistry.

After retirement, I thought, *What better way to test my intellectual capacities than making something I love?* In my case, this turned out to be wine. The catalyst that triggered everything happened on one of our many vacations to Napa Valley, just fifteen miles from where I was born. One afternoon during a winery tour, the winemaker said in describing the wine-making process, "You need to be a *scientist* to make a decent bottle of wine." By hearing that key word, I knew my intellectual challenge was set.

I'd always loved wine. In fact, for the past forty years, I've had two glasses for dinner each night. Growing up near Napa Valley, we had vines in our backyard. But the idea of growing grapes and making wine from scratch never once entered my mind until I retired. However, once I decided to put in a vineyard and build my own winery, I spared no expense and invested in the finest wine-making equipment, spraying devices, vineyard systems, barrels, packaging materials, and other equipment. If I was going to do this, I didn't want any excuses for not being able to do it right.

Luckily, I met the Johnny Appleseed of the San Diego vintner world, Pete Anderson, who became a dear friend. Pete knew every phase from vineyard installation to vineyard management, to harvesting into wine making, to packaging. With his expert guidance, this old scientist got to work.

THE GEREVAS FAMILY WINERY

There was so much I had to learn.

My wine-making journey started with testing the soil health and productivity of my land. It turned out I had to add potassium, calcium, and zinc because I had to make sure the soil pH was right. Then came the building and maintaining of the vineyard phase. Orchestrating the maturity of your grapes is exciting. However, having a vineyard is like having a restaurant. The only difference is you get a lot of uninvited hungry guests, including ants, bees, yellow jackets, beetles, birds, coyotes, deer, and potbellied pigs. (This last one was thanks to our neighbor who had a pet pig that loved my grapes.)

Harvest prep itself took almost a day of getting everything ready for friends and family. I always assigned each person to a specific job, such as picker, sorter, crusher, weigher, photographer, and washer. My wife took over the second half of the event, which was cooking a fabulous brunch for everyone with last year's wine being the key feature.

Since my wife is Italian and cooks unbelievable Italian food, I focused on making Italian wine. Sangiovese (Brunello) was the primary varietal, but I used some cabernet sauvignon, merlot, and cabernet franc for blending. Since I made Italian wine, I naturally needed to play Italian opera throughout the vineyard and winery during work and all tours. On quiet evenings, our entire neighborhood would hear Andrea Bocelli and Luciano Pavarotti. But no one complained because everyone knew they would be getting some of my wine.

The night before harvest, after a full day of preparation, I would take my last brix reading to make sure the grapes were ready. I'd pour a glass of last year's winning blend, put on some Italian opera, sit under a couple of beautiful Spanish olive trees I had planted, and just look at my babies ready to give their lives for tomorrow's celebration.

Once crushed, the scientist in me began to administer some common tests such as pH, titratable acidity, residual sugar, free SO_2, volatile acidity, and percent of alcohol. After fermentation there was the bottling, capping, and labeling party with some tasting of the final product. The two hundred bottles produced would go to harvesters, family, friends, and taste-testing events and parties.

THE WINE-TASTING GODS BLESS MY WINE

The wine-tasting world in America genuflects to only one person, Eddie Osterland. In 1973 Eddie became the first American to be anointed as a master sommelier—the highest distinction one can attain in the wine services category. Eddie is known by sommeliers around the world and gives speeches to thousands of corporate leaders every year at their annual events. He happens to live about fifteen miles from where I live and went to school with one of my former board members who talked him into doing a charity event for me.

Eddie agreed to do the event but only if I allowed him to come see my winery and taste my wine. I'm not sure how to describe what went through my mind when he asked if he could do this. It was like Tiger Woods asking if he could come over to the house to see my golf swing. Mind you this was only the second year my vines produced grapes, and normally you would not bottle your wine until the third year. But I was too anxious and even made wine the first year for practice and gave it to my gardener, mailman, pool guy, and electrician.

Ron holding the grapes, bottle, and gold medal from his "Best in Class" vintage

After showing Eddie my vines, we went into the winery to taste my wine from the barrel. I poured each of us a glass. Eddie put his up to the light, swirled it, sniffed it, put some in his mouth, and spit it out. Then he repeated the process and finally swallowed. He asked what I intended to do with the wine, and I said I planned to give it to the same crowd and throw the rest away.

"I wouldn't do that," he said. "Instead, I'd enter it in the county contest."

I smiled, thinking it was a joke. But then I realized he was serious and that I might be on to something. I entered my wine in the San Diego International Wine and Spirits Challenge, which is one of the oldest and most respected competitions in the US. Unbelievably, I won "Best in Class" along with a gold medal for my Sangiovese. I couldn't wait to call Eddie.

"You aren't going to believe what just happened," I said.

His response was classic. "Ron, what do you think I do for a living?"

Years after winning more of the same awards, I was introduced to the only master sommelier in all of New Zealand, Cameron Douglas—a terrific guy who remains a dear friend. It took him over six years to pass the master's wine test, which is not unusual, and he is clearly an expert. One afternoon, I had Cameron do a complete vertical tasting on all my wines, and to my surprise, he scored me much higher than I anticipated.

WINE EXPERIENCES

Going back to my days in executive search, my top wine industry search was for the president of Charles Krug Winery, the oldest working winery in Napa Valley and owned by the Mondavi family. Peter Mondavi, who passed away at 102 in 2016, was a dear friend. He looked forward to our annual visit and especially my wife's biscotti.

Ron and Rosalie with Peter Mondavi at the Charles Krug Winery, 2012

The Charles Krug Winery is across the road from the Culinary Institute of America in St. Helena, which conducts some of the finest classes on vineyard management and wine making anywhere on the planet. The best of the best are guest speakers and lecturers. My wife would buy me a weeklong class every year for my birthday, and we would use it as one of our vacation trips. In return, I would buy her a week or two in Italy every year, which included a couple of wineries on the itinerary.

Our vineyard was used for everything. I gave hundreds of wine-tasting tours and lectures. We even had a wedding where I married two good friends of ours in the vineyard. Then there was the dinner for eight that was auctioned off by the Serving Seniors charity for $5,000. This included a wine lecture and dinner at our home. The board chairwoman (Rosalie) and the VP of development were the chefs while yours truly gave a tour and wine-making talk to the group.

Instead of serving my wines for dinner, I surprised everyone by serving the Napa wines that won the 1976 Judgement of Paris contest—Stag's Leap Wine Cellars cab and Chateau Montelena Winery chardonnay. This contest put Napa on the world wine map as number one. As I poured the different wines, I narrated the history of each and their unique characteristics.

WINE WITH GOD

While challenging myself physically and intellectually was wonderful, the most fulfilling of my personal challenges was my spiritual pilgrimage.

I had always been spiritual but not very religious. I seldom went to church because I never enjoyed it. Whenever I attended Mass, it seemed there was never enough time to communicate with the Lord. By the time we all finished standing, kneeling, singing, praying, and listening to the sermon, it was time to leave. This routine always seemed too programmed, and it felt like I was just checking off a Sunday-box ritual.

So I decided to take matters into my own hands and make God a bigger part of my life. My home was on top of a hill, and I barbecued about every other night next to our swimming pool. Ever since my land navigation class in the military, I'd always loved astrology. In this setting, the stars seemed close enough for me to reach out and touch. Knowing that light travels at a speed of 186,000 miles per second and that the closest star is four light-years away, this always led me to think about heaven and God.

Realizing some of the burned-out stars I saw weren't even there but that it would still take years for their light to disappear made me realize how insignificant I was and how magnificent God is. This setting was perfect. Since I had two glasses of wine every night, I decided to start having my first one with God while I was barbecuing and walking through my vineyard and the other with my wife at dinner. No interruptions. Only the stars and my grapes. Since no one could hear me, the conversations were very personal and rather engaging. I'm using past tense because we recently downsized. Now it's roses instead of grapes. But I still have similar barbecue conversations with my wine and a lovely new view.

I must admit I feel awkward writing about my spirituality and communication with the Lord—especially in a book. But one of my goals in writing was to thank God for what he has given me and my family, and I'm not ashamed to do so publicly.

APPRECIATION OF LIFE GROWS WITH AGE

It's been interesting how the conversations and communication has changed over the years. In my seventies, the first decade of retirement, I was thankful for such a wonderful life and would say so often. But now that I'm in my eighties, I'm grateful for *each* new day. I fully realize that time is running out and that it's all gravy from this point on. After receiving so much, I'm embarrassed to ask for more but will continue to serve in any way I can (such as helping our veterans).

My wife and I thank God every day for what we have and have always said that what has made our journey so special is that we came from nothing and know how fortunate we have been. We also recognize that we did our part to earn it. That's one of the main reasons I'm writing this book. I know how much more the average person can achieve.

As a lover of music, I often need it to calm me down or take me elsewhere. There are only two songs on my desktop. One is "God Bless the U.S.A.," by Lee Greenwood and The Singing Sergeants, and the other is "Angels Among Us," by Tim Faust and Chris Rupp. No other song makes me appreciate my country or my life more than these, and I wish I had a nickel for every time I've played them.

I'm certainly biased, but I'm convinced I was born at the right time in our country's history. I'm lucky enough to say I've lived in all ten decades. And I'm thankful I grew up at a time when family, marriage, tradition, and country meant more than they do today.

STAYING INTELLECTUALLY ENGAGED IS ESSENTIAL

Retirement is not the time to stop growing. As American writer William S. Burroughs points out, "When you stop growing, you start dying." Although you may not wish to test your limitations like me, I strongly encourage you to stay intellectually engaged with what's happening around you and with those who are important to you.

One of the ways you can do this is through creatively using your expertise in new and exciting ways for more personal growth. A key reason I wanted to teach was to remain current with younger generations and stay relevant with the future leaders of our country.

Another way I leveraged my expertise was to join the Prague Leadership Institute (PLI) Board in the Czech Republic. PLI was created by my former partner, Pepper de Callier, to help the Eastern European block of countries become more sophisticated in Western World leadership practices. I served on the faculty of PLI and consulted with Prague leaders to help them understand the use-and-effect relationship between the human element of leadership and the bottom-line performance of their business and themselves.

The highlight of my work in Europe was being asked to participate in Forum 2000. It is recognized as one of Europe's most prestigious leadership events and involves leaders from all over the world. Vaclav Havel, the former president of the Czech Republic and leader of the 1989 Velvet Revolution, chaired the event. I spoke on corporate social responsibility, and Madeleine Albright, former US secretary of state, gave the keynote address. She was very good but fell short of the prior year's speaker, the Dalai Lama.

Another totally unexpected new, fun, and lucrative opportunity presented itself because of my expertise in executive search. After I retired, I agreed to serve as a legal expert in one of the biggest corporate employment lawsuits ever. I was hired to serve as a team member of a well-known global accounting firm defending itself against former officers of one of the major US telecommunications companies. This involved six full months of work in preparation for trial.

When it was over, the lead attorney called to thank me and said, "Ron, we are indeed grateful as you helped save us at least $200 million, so thank you. But let me give you a piece of advice. Next time charge more for your services. Your counterpart that competed against you on the other team charged $200 an hour more than you did." I found that very interesting since I charged $600 per hour. In any case, as you see, it pays off to specialize and become an expert.

There are endless ways for you to continue to grow your intellectual capacity during retirement. You just have to be willing to take advantage of them when they arise and find new opportunities for yourself.

FAMILY FIRST

Now, we get to my favorite part because I saved the best for last.

My family has always come first with me. In my mind, if you aren't successful in raising your family, nothing else matters. If you've had a good role model to follow, your job as a parent is much easier. If not, you are forced to learn with your partner and hope for the best. There is no more important job than parenting, and yet, most of it is discovered by on-the-job training.

Family gathering, Christmas 2006

Rosalie and I are lucky to have two great kids. We had our moments to be sure, but no serious or permanent problems that altered the course of their lives. Fortunately, both of our kids chose terrific partners, and we look forward to our annual international vacations with Michelle and our son-in-law, Dana. Plus, it's convenient having our son and daughter-in-law, Mary Kate, less than an hour away and to watch our granddaughter, Sophia, grow up.

Working with my son was one of the greatest joys of my life. Getting him started in his career was amazing. Being his baseball coach and doing marathons and triathlons together were special for both of us. I'm very proud of his professional achievements but love how terrific he is as a father and husband. It'll be interesting to see how far away he allows his daughter to go to college because Rosalie and I had a horrible time when we dropped him off at college less than an hour away from home. Minutes after pulling away, we had to pull off the road so we could cry together like a couple of babies!

Ron, Rosalie, and granddaughter Sophia

His daughter, Sophia, our only grandchild, has been the center-piece of our family for the past ten years. My wife, of course, would like to have a dozen more. But Sophia fills the bill nicely. I have a special art piece above my computer that says, "I love you, Gramps my BFF." And I look at it whenever I need a little boost. Her parents are doing a great job of raising a lovely young lady who I love a ton.

I'm sure you have a sense of how I feel about my daughter, Michelle, and what our relationship is from reading her foreword in this book. It's been wonderful watching my little girl grow into such a lovely woman. I honestly believe every dad should have a daughter to fully understand what unconditional love is. Not that I don't possess it for my wife and son, but it is different for your baby girl. I never knew how many different protective instincts I possessed until she moved through each stage of life.

She was my first student, and I've enjoyed a mentoring relationship with her throughout her entire career. Now we mentor each other. For almost twenty years, we would run every weekend and have breakfast afterward. Career development was the main subject of our conversation. Her dream job was to work for Qualcomm, but since it was the biggest and best corporation in San Diego, there were only fifty thousand other individuals who had the same objective.

It took us almost five years to accomplish this mission. But that was over eighteen years and three promotions ago. Some executives are very happy with their company and job. Some even love their work. And then there is Michelle. Suffice it to say that all those miles, omelets, and plans paid off beautifully.

Last, but certainly not least, is the woman I've been married to for the past fifty-seven years. The first person I ever hired, the first person I ever promoted, and the first and only person I ever married. My nineth commandment starts with "Your Life Partner Can Make a Big Difference." I can assure you this is definitely true. A healthy, productive, loving marriage has never been easy to achieve. And I would submit that more is required today to accomplish the same as yesterday. More options and flexibility exist, but the world is changing at a speed that makes it more challenging just to keep pace.

If your partner needs the same kinds of basic things you do to be happy, it helps. In our case, the chalk lines were clear. Neither one of us had *anything*, but both wanted *something* and were willing to work for it. Our folks saw to it that we both graduated with a college education and a strong work ethic. That's all we needed. They did their jobs. We did the rest and appreciated what we earned every step of the way.

Since family was number one for both of us, Rosalie clearly had the most important job to start our journey. I just had to go be as successful as I possibly could so that when she was ready to do her thing, we would have the flexibility and options for her to do what she wanted to do. I had little fear that when the time came, she could make the adjustment because the good Lord dealt her more intellectual cards than me.

She didn't waste much time. As soon as she gave birth to our first child, she joined an aerobic dancing class to stay fit. By the time she delivered our second child three years later, she was the Los Angeles area manager for Jacki Sorensen's aerobic dancing organization and in charge of more than a hundred instructors and five thousand students. It was here that she had her first fundraising experience when she raised over $100,000 in one day for the Special Olympics in 1984.

This experience ignited a fire that has been burning for the past forty years. It has resulted in a series of leadership positions and achievements in charitable work and volunteer service. In fact, Rosalie was recently selected as Chairwoman for the 2024 Salvation Army Women of Dedication event. Over six hundred people will attend next year's event, which will recognize twelve women leaders in the

San Diego community. Rosalie received this prestigious honor ten years ago.

Along the way, she was president of the San Diego affiliate of the Susan G. Komen Breast Cancer Foundation and chair of their Race for the Cure for four years, board chair of Serving Seniors for four years, and president of the Women's Auxiliary for the Salvation Army in San Diego. She also serves on the Metropolitan Board for the Salvation Army and is on the advisory board for Vision of Children Foundation.

The amazing thing is that she shows no signs of slowing down. Both of our goal lists seem to be getting longer by the day. And you know what? We wouldn't have it any other way.

My wife often says she wouldn't have ever done all of this if it hadn't been for me. And I am quick to say the same goes for me. Both statements, I believe, are true. We have far exceeded our expectations, and both made sacrifices for the good of the team. Along the way, we learned to enjoy and appreciate the other's priorities.

When it came time for Rosalie to assume leadership responsibilities and board roles, like most who have never done it, she needed a little push and some mentoring. I knew exactly what I was helping create, and it didn't take much prompting. But I take pride in what help I was able to offer.

I've often heard someone who is married question if they chose the right partner. After all, what signs exist to help answer that question? While everyone's story is different, in our case, a small hint occurred last week from a neighbor. We live in a gated community of sixty homes with three winding hill streets that many of the residents walk almost every day for exercise and neighborly chat. Last week another couple stopped Rosalie and me to chat and said with a smile, "Regardless of how far away we see you two, we always know it's the

Gerevases because they are the only couple that hold hands everywhere they walk." That's our story.

I have always felt an obligation to provide career advice to my family first and foremost, especially when giving career advice is my profession and passion. But I would go further and say *all* parents have an obligation to share more than just "the birds and bees" part of life with their children. They should share what they have learned about work and responsibilities. Or they should refer them to another relative or friend that can help them in ways they cannot.

Very few things in life bring as much joy as knowing you have played some small part in helping someone be successful and happy, especially when it's a member of your family. In my eyes, this is the greatest change one can ever make.

EPILOGUE

I never intended to write a book. Originally, I just planned to list a few dates and tell a few career stories for our children. But as I thought through my life, I knew I wanted to write my story on paper. One of the reasons is I've never discussed most of these events with even my closest friends and family members. We always talked about what *they* were doing or what *we* were doing.

I still think back to my time in the Peace Corps when my son Stephen's preschool teacher asked him what his daddy did for work. Stephen's response? "He rides the bus!" In his little world, that was all he saw. He watched his daddy get on in the morning and return at night. Yes, my kids knew I flew all over the world, but they did not know where I went or what I did. Besides, I always found their lives much more interesting.

Another reason I wanted to tell my story is because our family tree is running out of branches, and I wanted there to be a record of our last three generations. I also saw it as another way of reaching more people with my message. And to be honest, I wanted to write it down before I forgot.

BE A CHANGE AGENT

A final word to you, my dear readers. Most of us don't get a chance to change much in this world because most of us don't like change. A few of us like to change everything we touch. But only some of us succeed.

I have spent most of my working life trying to be a change agent in every organization I joined. While most people would be content to add minor contributions to their businesses, my aim was to directly impact the number one or number two companies in size and reputation within their industry. Why? Because if you change *one* of the industry's leaders for the better, you can impact an entire industry. Yes, this is ambitious, but it's been how I measured success.

As a result, I helped make a historical change in four different industry leaders, and these changes are still integral to their operations today. I left the best job in my life to change a fifth but was prevented from doing so for both internal and external reasons. And I was prevented from implementing my sixth, and most important new business model, because of federal government politics.

As my book title suggests, I have been relentless in trying to improve the careers of as many people as possible. However, the purpose in writing this book was to inspire you to make changes that would help you exceed whatever your current expectations might be.

While I've witnessed time and again how easy it is for others to exceed their career expectations, too many of us underestimate our potential. I've seen this up close in the classes I've taught and even closer with colleagues over the years. If you get nothing else from this book but this message, it will be time worth spent. You owe it to yourself and your family to use the gifts that you have been given.

KEEP DREAMING AND CREATE YOUR OWN PERSONAL COMMANDMENTS

Just because I'm eighty-five doesn't give me any excuse to stop dreaming. I still have a long list of goals I want to achieve:

- Sell as many books as possible since all proceeds go to veterans.

- Help as many readers advance their careers as possible.

- Continue to prepare students and veterans for career success.

- Create as many new Change Agents as possible.

- Help my USA Triathlon Team win a world championship.

- Help someone implement my Veterans Career Network model.

- Make one more bottle of award-winning Italian wine.

- Learn how to be closer God.

- Learn how to play pickleball.

Dreaming keeps us young and hungry. It also helps us avoid the temptation to stagnate. While there are certain lists, such as my Ten Career Commandments in chapter 8 that define how I work with others, there is another list that drives me personally. While the details of this list could fill another book, I'll share a summary of these to hopefully inspire you to action.

The first is to put yourself in the place of others when you speak to them. It's easy to assume, but it's best to listen. Learning how to be empathetic is critical.

Second, we underestimate daily organization and prioritization at our peril. It pays to be efficient and effective. Remember my suggestion to take five minutes each night and prioritize your next day.

Third, timing is everything. I'm convinced the good Lord put me in the right place at the right time to make a difference. And this inner knowledge of how fortunate I was resulted in an unusual level of appreciation and positive reinforcement. The same is true with you. I believe there is a reason you have the opportunities you have, so make the most of them.

Fourth, I remain convinced that *every* person or group of people can be improved. There is nothing that cannot be changed for the better. And if you take this approach in life and in business, you will have a successful career.

Fifth, the more effectively I learned how to compartmentalize my frustration and pain, the more efficient I was in stressful situations, and the better decisions I made. This point is critical. Life throws us unexpected curveballs that seek to knock us flat. But it's up to us to respond the right way.

Sixth, I chose to display my leadership skills and instincts in meetings. Maybe one day I'll write a book titled *Ronald's Rules of Order* because I believe my ability to conduct productive meetings was one of the greatest contributors to my success. I never entered a meeting unprepared. I always knew the key questions and issues that would be discussed and had already placed myself in the position of my toughest critics. It is essential that you make sure time in meetings is time well spent. Otherwise, don't have them.

And seventh, nice guys don't have to come in last. In *Career Trek* Professor Troy Nielsen writes, "Find your fit, pursue your passion, and share your smile."[21] He goes on to say, "There has perhaps never been a more important time in our nation's history for people to rediscover

---

21   Troy Nielsen, *Career Trek* (Saddle River: Prentice Hall, 2007).

their smile and strive to find true meaning and joy in their lives."[22] He wrote that over fifteen years ago, and it's still appropriate today.

These characteristics are what separated me from the crowd, but it's up to you to create your own. You might not shine in meetings, but there might be another space where you do. Perhaps you're not the most organized person on the planet, but you can get better. There might be times when you think, *Who am I to be a change agent at my organization?* But in these moments, trust your abilities and lean into your strengths.

CREATE YOURSELF

George Bernard Shaw was right when he said, "Life isn't about finding yourself. Life is about creating yourself."

I've faced a lot of tough organizational challenges, and not once did I have a predetermined solution for how to solve them. Instead, I always found the answers the same way and from the same sources. I found out what our customers wanted and then listened to those in our organization delivering our product. By taking these two steps, I was able to create the changes everyone desired.

Being a change agent doesn't happen by accident. It requires a strategic, methodical approach. In fact, if you were to look back on the ten chapters in this book, you'll notice how each change naturally leads into the next.

Chapter 1 pointed out that everything starts with changing yourself. If you're not willing to change, don't expect to change others. This involves having the right mindset.

Chapter 2 focused on changing your horizons. Just as my time in college broadened my view of the world, you need to have key experi-

---

22   Ibid.

ences that enlarge your vision. Ask yourself, *Am I willing to stretch the boundaries of my comfort zone?*

Chapter 3 reminds you why it's so important to change your focus. It's great to do a bunch of wonderful things, but at some point you need to home in on those things you're really good at. And sometimes it takes a timely conversation, like mine with Dean Benz, to steer you in the right direction.

Chapter 4 challenged you to change your standards. Arriving at J. Walter Thompson, there was so much I didn't know. But there was one thing I did and that was that I needed to up my game. I needed to learn what it took to become a professional. Without learning this lesson, there was no way I could have made any of the changes that followed.

Chapter 5 centered on changing your impact. Arriving in DC and operating as an apolitical Republican in a Democrat town was challenging. But despite living in an era of turbulent Watergate politics, I demonstrated it was possible to do a lot of good, even under a cloud of bad. You, too, can make impactful change even in the toughest situations.

Chapter 6 brought you into the heart of this book and the importance of changing your career. After three decades in the executive search industry, I became more convinced than ever that change is possible, specialization is key, and developing the right network of connections is critical to success. The same will likely be true with you.

Chapter 7 took you from focusing on your career to changing your industry. Ultimately, when your career is stable, the larger question you should ask is, *How can I create change that raises the tide of all boats?* At this point, you're thinking beyond yourself and how to maximize your value to others.

Chapter 8 was about giving back to students. And while you might not teach at a university, there are countless ways you can give back. Ask yourself, "Who are some people I can mentor today?" Maybe it's a coworker or friend. Maybe volunteering your time to a local charity. But the key is to find ways to give back, just as others have given to you.

Chapter 9 was different, and it revealed my ongoing passion for veterans. This is a change that still needs to be done, and maybe you might be the one to make it happen!

Chapter 10 revealed the three realities in life I think are most important. These include a good relationship with the Lord, a strong physical body, and a vibrant intellectual capacity. As I've discovered, each of these areas can be nurtured and developed. It doesn't matter how old you are. Retirement isn't a time to kick back. It's a time to get going!

Notice how each of these changes build upon the one before. I couldn't change my horizons before I changed myself. I couldn't change my impact before I changed my standards. And I couldn't change my industry before I changed my career. Change starts within and then gradually trickles out to those around us.

So, with this in mind, I challenge you to become a change agent. Yes, you might have some doubts about making the changes you know need to be made. But in the words of the second-century Greek philosopher Epictetus, "How long are you going to wait until you demand the best of yourself?"

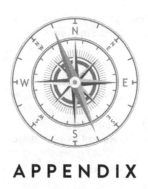

APPENDIX

(A) VETERANS CAREER NETWORK—PROCESSES

	TASK	ACTUAL	PROTOTYPE
1	Create interest profile including living preferences	Marine answers questions online using adaptive question sequence; creates interest profile	Answers questions; simulate adaptive using multiple rounds of questioning
2	Match interest profile with military and civilian job activities and requirements	Computer performs database match on "standard" military profile items	Manually match interests with military and civilian job activities and requirements
3	Verify interest and location preferences; update interest profile	Marine answers questions online re: profile mismatches, conflicts, incompletes; updates interest profile	Interview with marine to clarify mismatches, conflicts, and incompletes
4	Create list of potential job categories for review	Computer displays top (eight) job category matches	Paper presentation of what would be on computer screen
5	Review the list and gather more information	Marine clicks on job category, which displays write-up, pictures, and video of vets holding jobs in that category	Marine reviews folder with write-up pictures and link to vets video for each job

6	Talk with vet(s) currently holding job category of top interest	Set up and conduct a Zoom interview with the vet holding the job category	Set up and conduct a Zoom interview with vet holding job
7	Update interest profile by indicating relative like/dislike of job category attributes and living preference	Marine enters simple Likert-scale questions on job activities and living preferences relevant to job category, updating weighting factors	Marine answers simple Likert-scale paper-pencil questions on job activities and living preferences
8	Create list of employers' open jobs category in preferred living location	Computer performs database match on job category and living location	Manually search open jobs in job category in San Diego North County
9	Review list of top potential jobs for review and gather more information	Computer displays top (three) employers and positions matching; marine clicks on job, which displays company write-up, pictures, and maybe video	Present marine list of top (three) employers and positions; marine reviews folder with company write-up, pictures, and video for each job
10	Make tentative decision on first choice, send request for Zoom interview	Marine enters decision on first choice; email is generated to company asking for Zoom interview, marine résumé, and profile attached to email	Marine makes decision on first choice; email is sent to company asking for Zoom interview; create marine résumé and profile in Word
11	Conduct Zoom interview	Computer generates a suggested set of interview questions for both marine and business; marine and business conduct Zoom interview	Create suggested set of interview questions with marine and business and give to both
12	Make decision on pursuing further and provide feedback to both; schedule onsite visit	Marine and company make decision to pursue further; if either do not, audio record reasons and send to the other	Marine and company make decision to pursue further; if either do not, audio record reasons and send to the other
13	Conduct onsite visit	Conduct onsite visit	Conduct onsite visit
13a	Determine further education needs	Computer generates list of job skill mismatches and send to marine and business via email	Create list of job skill mismatches and send to marine and business via email

(B) VETERANS CAREER NETWORK—PROCESS CHART

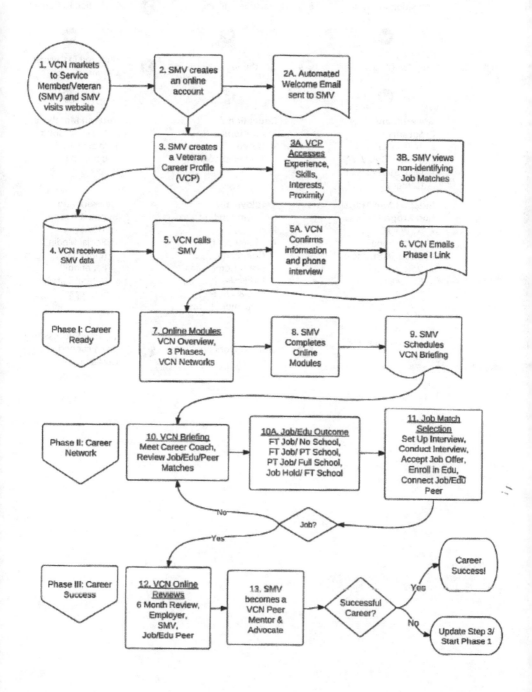

MILITARY TO CIVILIAN CAREER TRANSITION MATRIX

Transition Step	Transition to Civilian	❯	Transition to Job	❯	Transition to Career
	⌄		⌄		⌄
Objective	Prep for The Job	❯	Get the Job	❯	Succeed in Civilian Career
	⌄		⌄		⌄
Entities	**Government Programs** • TAP – DoD • VOW – DoD / VA • ONe Stop Career Centers **Independent Transition Programs** • REBOOT Workshops • Boots in Business • Veterans Job Success		**Educational Institutions** • Colleges • Trade Schools **Employment** (Veteran Job Success Partners) • Chambers of Commerce • Local Companies • Industries (Power, Gas & Oil, etc) • Placement Firms		**Veteran Members** • In Similar Jobs • In similar companies **Network and Support Groups** • MEA • Social Media (LinkedIn, Facebook) • Veteral Career Success
Result	Veteran "Ready for Hire"	❯	Veteran Working	❯	Veteran Successfully Transistioned to a Civilian Career

GET IN CONTACT WITH RON

If you want to speak with Ron about your career, you can reach **him** through rongerevas.com.